SOME HORSES

Books by Thomas McGuane

The Sporting Club

The Bushwhacked Piano

Ninety-two in the Shade

Panama

An Outside Chance

Nobody's Angel

Something to Be Desired

To Skin a Cat

Keep the Change

Nothing but Blue Skies

Some Horses

SOME HORSES

Thomas McGuane

The Lyons Press

Illustrations by Buckeye Blake

Designed by A Good Thing Inc.
10 9 8 7 6 5 4 3 2 1

FIRST EDITION

Library of Congress Cataloging-in-Publication Data

McGuane, Thomas.
    Some Horses / Thomas McGuane.
        p.   cm.
    ISBN 1-55821-891-2
    1. Horses.   I. Title
SF301.M45   1999
636.1′088′6—dc21   98-56057
                                                    CIP

Some of these essays originally appeared in *Sports Illustrated*, *Men's Journal*, *The Atlantic Monthly*, *Outside*, *Texas Monthly*, and *Harper's*.

for Buster Welch

CONTENTS

1
HORSES

Those who love horses are impelled by an ever-receding vision, some enchanted transformation through which the horse and the rider become a third, much greater thing. No such image haunts the dreams of the motorist. Becoming one with your car is the subject of perhaps unforeseen comedy. The dream of animals is counterpoised by the nightmare that our inventions will turn on us. This is the age of the machine and all things of flesh are imperiled by it, especially that terrible machine of transportation the automobile, which has ruined our towns, our countryside, and perhaps our families. The geopolitics of oil, the murderous disquiet of the oil-producing regions owe their unhappiness to the need to fuel that thing that replaced the horse. The humblest horse owner with a cherished animal in the backyard is doing his or her part to help the spirit travel in a more bountiful way.

3

Somehow, in the last thirty years, my life has filled up with horses and with other animals as well, dogs certainly, numerous barn cats, several wonderful cockatiels, the wild animals we live among, some of whom have become habituated to us. We are particularly aware of nearby annual nesters, the red-tailed hawks, the golden eagles, the all-knowing ravens, and the bird for whom Montanans have an ironic and amused affection, the magpie. Animals seem to belong to a family from which only man is estranged.

I bought a small ranch in the 1960s and over the last several decades it has moved and enlarged. Living on a ranch was my choice but my four children simply grew up that way, going from one-room schools to the state university. Horses were always around, always, in the view of others, too many of them. Now the children are grown and gone but my wife and I are not alone. The horses are still here.

Horses occupy a special place because they require so much care, and because they are curiously fragile, possess the prey species' excessive faith in the value of flight. A friend of mine in Oklahoma said to me, "God made a perfect world but he would like one chance to redesign the horse." Certainly, some work could be done with feet, hocks, suspensory tendons, navicular bones, all of which seem far too delicate for the speed and weight of the horse. And too often, the fifty feet of unsupported intestine acquires a simple loop and kills the horse. If the horse were a Ford, the species would vanish beneath lawsuits engendered by consumer-protection laws.

I've sometimes wondered why I've spent so much time with horses. In the past, I was quite happy with mice. I had several lovely ones. I see nearly as much in their pert whiskers and beady eyes as I do in million-dollar Northern Dancer yearlings. But because of its size, the horse imposes its moods and ways upon us. My wife and I have occasionally considered bringing our horses into the house so that they could see exactly where we live but have declined out of concern that they would find some of our more doubtful possessions, our television, say, or the telephone, so alarming that they would express their disapproval by destroying furniture and walls. Who would blame them?

Size doesn't tell the whole story but I've occasionally envied the East Indians whose lives are given to the care of elephants, whose size says something about the consent by animals to the very existence of the fast-breeding turbo-monkey called man. If you think of animals as humanity and mankind as the lawyers, you get my picture.

We have saturated the horse with our emotions. In silent movies, the hero was identified by having him give a lump of sugar to a horse. The horse provided the only genuineness in the film and was used to certify the actors. The Amish Standardbreds who pull carriages in Central Park have learned what most humans cannot: parallel parking. Their quiet obedience exists in eerie contrast to the agitated city. The horses I saw in the BLM mustang corrals at Rock Springs, Wyoming, whirling, running with every muscle, every vein in sculptural exaggeration, were so alarmed at being swept from the mountain hiding places by government helicopters they seemed bent on mass suicide. But we humans, hanging from the woven wire fence surrounding them, just wanted to be closer to them. My uncles joined the Boston mounted police because it was the only way they could afford to have a horse. Brendan Behan contemptuously defined the Anglo-Irishman as "a Protestant with a horse."

To some people, horses have wings. Horses took the Sioux out of the Minnesota woods. In Montana's Pryor Mountains, they've found horse skeletons with the extra vertebrae of the Spaniards' Moorish steeds, reproachful bones in the hills above the oil refineries. The U.S. Cavalry lost control of the confiscated hunting horses of the Plains Indians whenever buffalo appeared on the horizon: the horses struck free and surrounded the bison though their riders had vanished from their backs forever. The great scholar of the Northern Plains Indians Vern Deusenberry said that the principal point of the Battle of the Little Big Horn was that it was the end of the buffalo culture. It was also the end of the completely free-roaming horsemen of North America, and maybe of the world.

In the American West, the horse is considered part of a sacred birthright even though the native westerner is no more likely to be a horseman than is an Ohioan or a New Yorker. In the case of populous western states like Texas, he is perhaps less likely. Here in Montana, the most effete native condo dweller will chuckle at an out-of-stater on a horse. But a lover of horses has nothing to prove and no expertise to reveal. It is important that we find animals to love, and that is the end of the story.

It is bootless to argue for the horse in terms of his usefulness. By modern pragmatic standards, the Sarmations of the ancient Hungarian plains are the only people to have utilized horses fully: they rode them, ate them, drank their blood, made armor out of their hooves, and sacrificed them to their gods.

It is not the duty of the horse to be a biofeedback mechanism for yearning humans; yet it is remarkable how consistently people with horses claim to have learned much about themselves through them. Certainly, the management of a horse will give you a rapid evaluation of your patience, your powers of concentration, and your ability to hold on to delicate ideas for sustained periods of time.

My own horsemanship is peculiar to the country I ride in and the technical limitations of my riding. I can only respect, ignorantly and from afar, the refinements of English riding, fox hunting, jumping, dressage. I know nothing important about them beyond that they must not be easy to master. I will go a long way to watch real stadium jumpers and, because my daughter Annie rides them, reining horses. I am particularly interested in the bridle horses of California. Theirs is an ancient art conveyed from the time of Spanish rule and there is a solemn romance about these horses with their swan necks, their Santa Barbara Spanish bridles, their lightning quickness, and the steady whir of the rollers in their bits.

The country available to me permits me to ride farther than anyone is likely to wish to take a horse. I can go to Wyoming from my home in Montana without crossing a road and I have hundreds of square miles of easily accessed wild foothills. I am a wanderer in any case but I prefer inarticulate companionship. Horses and dogs are ideal and I often go with both. The biggest limitation for dogs in my region is the prevalence of rattlesnakes in the warm months. Despite precaution, all of my dogs have been bitten by them and all have recovered. The greatest safety for a dog in snake country at the 45th parallel is to be larger than forty pounds; beyond this size it is nearly impossible for a snake to kill one. Actually, horses are in greater danger, as they are sometimes bitten in the nose while grazing: when their passages close, they suffocate because they are unable to breathe through their mouths. Native horses are alert to snakes and I have several times had them abruptly sidepass in the backcountry; it is only when I looked behind us and saw the coiled reptile that I understood the meaning of the sudden movement. My wonderful old mare Sunday Bomb could see a snake from a half mile. The horses we haven't raised have come from Texas and they are well up on snake. They always see them before I do.

I have gone up a mountain trail on a horse, after a year's absence, and had the horse snort and stare in suspicion at a place where a tree has been removed since the horse's last visit, a tree among millions. The phenomenal alertness to space, shape, smell, and light amount to a kind of capacity, if you are unwilling to call it intelligence, beyond the human.

Forty years ago I came off a wild, stormy mountain in the middle of the night in Wyoming. I had no idea where I was, could not even see the ground. The horse took me home. The only thing I can remember was the sense of complete isolation, the horse's shoes sparking beneath me on the granite rocks and the quiet arrival without a stumble to disturb our passage.

Training a horse then becomes an exploration of the horse's capacity for logic and muscle memory, logic being little more than doing this to avoid that. Trained performance horses are frequently loped for hours before the competition so that all they have left is muscle memory and they are unlikely to get chaotic personal ideas that send them off pattern, at least in human terms. For example, we require cutting horses to stop and turn on their haunches. It is our theory that this is the best way to hold and turn with a cow. It's probably not true. Buffalo and other wild cattle throw their rear quarters around and turn on their front ends. A model of speed and efficiency, the Argentine polo horse turns on his front end. The old "Texas style" polo horse that turns on his hindquarters is a thing of the past: his method of turning around was judged inefficient. A cutting horse under pressure or otherwise anxious is liable to forget the enforcement of the human idea and turn on his front end; therefore, he is galloped to a state of weariness, whereupon such big ideas do not occur. It is well to understand that this sort of turnaround simply looks right to us. More legitimately, a horse turning on its rear end is far easier to ride and less likely to spill with its rider. But we compel the horse see it our way.

The quiet, circumspect horseman makes every movement and even every thought around a green horse a building block of restraint and confidence. The best horsemen are quiet and consistent, firmly kind, and, from the horse's point of view, good listeners. An even temper is essential. Horses are capable of doing repetitious, annoying things, all of which can be corrected by a knowledgeable horseman who is patient enough to know that the correction may have to go on in very thin layers, like good varnish. Once when I watched Buster Welch, a cutting-horse trainer of whom I will have more to say, schooling my horse Sugar, I was surprised to see him let her drop her shoulder into her turn on the right side, producing a lunging and ineffective turnaround. "Aren't you going to ask her to quit that?" I asked. "Yes," said Buster, "but not all at once."

He knew how much she could absorb. Asking a horse to absorb more than it is capable of results in the excess being translated into anxiety. Anxiety in a horse can spread like a virus. Once it has, it sets the training back severely. Every trainer of dogs and horses knows that a year's work can be lost in a single moment of anger. It is decidedly better to err on the side of asking too little. The greatest error in training horses lies in not showing up for work often enough and trying to accomplish too much when you do.

In his disquisition on horsemanship, Xenophon, the Greek soldier-historian, emphasized patience and kindness in training the horse—"Never deal with him when you are in a fit of passion"—as the only approach that produces a finished and reliable horse, by which he meant a war horse, intended to carry a cuirassed rider into the chaos of armed strife. A horse trained for this was treated with the careful feeding and grooming—

including the provision of a special sandbox in which to roll—of the most pampered 4-H pony and all toward a mount upon whom one's life must depend. Xenophon's advice has not lost its usefulness in twenty-four hundred years. What he knew was based on long hours horseback; in one war, he traveled three thousand miles on his horse, fighting much of the way. Under such circumstances horse and rider would have few secrets from each other and it is heartening that Xenophon's conviction was one of deep respect.

For everyday riding, I require a surefooted horse. Some otherwise good horses, and frequently arena horses, are not particularly surefooted in the hills. They can improve but it is better if they grew up running in rough country. Surefootedness is important to me because I often ride alone, I get into some pinched spots, and I don't wear a helmet. Moreover, it is not a pleasure to ride a stumbling, woodenfooted horse who threatens life and limb in hard country. Ideally, a ranch horse ought to do a job but I ride far more than ranch work requires. Buster Welch feels that a horse should always be ridden with a purpose and if there isn't one then the rider should make one up: pick out a windmill on the horizon and ride straight to it. I'm not always successful in remembering this and sometimes go where the horse feels like going or just wander around looking for birds. However, horses definitely respond to this purposeful riding. I have ridden both field-trial dog horses and mustanging horses, and their drive to meet their objectives, to follow the hunt or to surmount a far hill to improve the view of the action, is something that comes right up through the seat of the rider's pants. Those who have not experienced a horse urgently going somewhere are unaware of their real physical capacity. That is why runaways are so blinding, so explosive. A runaway is far more dangerous than a downright bucking bronc as he becomes intoxicated by his speed and his adrenaline is transformed to rocket fuel.

If you ride in the backcountry alone, you also want a horse that will not come undone if a two-hundred-pound mule deer sails out from under you when you are pushing through the brush. Or, worse, a ten-bird covey of noisy little partridges. I have had some nastily thrilling experiences on arena-contest horses making their first rural rides, experiences that make the hyperbole about sitting on a keg of dynamite seem plausible. A good country horse should let you hang all sorts of things on the saddle—binoculars, a check cord for your dog, a slicker—and should not have any obvious fears, like that of moving water. Some young horses will break in two when the wind blows their tails up under them; some boil over with fear at the sight of anything new. A friend of mine who suffered a stroke and spent a couple of months in northern Montana at a rehabilitation center said the place was full of head-injured horsemen. Riding horses is not the place for baseless courage or hero-ism. A kind of earned confidence is what is required though it may run against the institutional inanity that validates foolhardy behavior. I have often no-ticed that good horsemen are like good sailors, meticulously and quietly tending to one detail after another, all to keep things running smoothly and safely. Once when I was watching Buster train horses, I sat crossways on my saddle, my knee crooked over the saddle horn, as was my habit. Buster stopped his training, rode over to me, and said, "Don't sit that way. It's dangerous." I don't do it anymore.

It is a pleasant thing to have a horse that will ground-tie, though the adage that a ground-tied horse is a loose horse is probably best kept firmly in mind. Some very fine horses will not stay with you if turned loose; they go home to their friends. Herd instinct is a constant magnetism, the early stages of what in, its more annoying form, is called "barn sour." My young mare Sass is the sort that will stay with me. She has no insecurity and is happy to be with me on an adven-ture. She loves to graze and, so far, it appears that when I drop the reins, she will stay near. Most, how-ever, will step on the reins and break them, sooner or later, then wander off. I hate losing nice, broken-in, pliant reins and prefer to let the horse drag a halter rope, which will usually cause a departing horse to stumble enough that it can be caught; but smart older horses learn to drag the rope to one side and can even lope that way. I have seen southern horsemen tie a cotton scale weight to their lead shank, a weight they must carry on the saddle betweentimes—usually a trooper's saddle with all sorts of handy rings—and this works quiet well. Another method is to put a snap on one rein so that the horse's head can be pulled around and snapped to the D-ring on the back cinch, causing the horse to circle. I have never tried this but I am aware that the horse eventually makes it clear to the rider that it is ready to be trusted and the snap can be dispensed with. There are lots of ways to try these things but it's important to imagine the consequences of the horse leaving and plan for them.

General tolerance is a great trait in a saddle horse. Our border collie Ella was a sweet and useful dog, usually out of shape for our fall cattle drive, and it was often necessary to pick her up when she got overheated or exhausted and throw her over the neck of my horse. Ella was quite unabashed when worn out and would come up to my stirrup and stand on her hind legs to be picked straight up from the ground and onto the horse, where she amiably took in the cattle drive from a moving and elevated point of observation. My horses went along with this even when she dug in with her claws to keep from toppling over the side. I ride a big, solid gelding named Zip, a great horse to ranch on, and he has had many miles of it. One day my neighbor came over with his three-year-old boy and the little boy demanded to sit on Zip. I lifted him aboard and Zip panicked, snorting, running backward, and preparing to bolt. I was lucky to snatch the child out of the saddle before a disaster occurred. There was a side of Zip I didn't know after hundreds of saddlings.

As between people, there is chemistry, good and bad, between the horse and its rider. We have a ranch gelding named Jack who regards me with anxious suspicion; he slings his head willfully when my wife rides and would prefer going to the barn. The last time I saw my daughter Annie riding him, she was standing on his bare back sailing along under the willow trees, both of them pictures of contented absorption. They have treated each other with benign mutual acceptance from the first moment they met. It happens.

As I have gotten older I have grown less interested in contests for horses and more interested in horses in general. I am very interested in untrained horses, such as yearlings and two-year-olds. There are few things more exciting than releasing a band of young horses from a corral where they have been confined for some time into open space and watching the explosion of movement as these meteors take on open country. This is sufficiently intoxicating to them that one must anticipate the collisions that they, in their understandable euphoria, sometimes fail to take into account. In Montana, wire cuts are called "education marks" but many a good horse has caused its own death in barbed wire and it must be watched vigilantly where horses are held.

On our somewhat marginal cattle ranch, the greatest pleasure is in moving cattle horseback at spring turnout, changing pastures throughout the grass season and the fall roundup. Some horses have a special aptitude for this work, moving steadily, anticipating herd quitters, willing to plunge into bad places to flush out cattle. When cattle are strung out in front of the horses for a long move, some of the drover sorcery can be felt, some of the enchantment I feel driving home from town when I pass the sign to the west of my ranch, OPEN RANGE. There's little of that left in the West but it may still account for most of the interest. There is an almost Homeric quality about the open-range books, Andy Adams's, *Log of a Cowboy* and Teddy "Blue" Abbott's *We Pointed Them North,* that is absent in the literature of the ranch. The avalanche of farm-and-ranch memoirs that pour, because of lack of general interest in them, from tax-supported university presses are mostly dull. The story possibilities of enclosed land are limited. The open range, the open sea, the open sky, the open wounds of the heart, that's where writers shine.

William Cobbett's *Rural Rides* wouldn't have its charm and power without the horse. The little stallion in Tolstoy's *Master and Man* is one of the best characters in the story and the greatest sacrifice to Tolstoy's tragic art. The boys that take the band of horses to the country during fly season in Turgenev's immortal *Bhezin Meadow* share the companionship and destiny of their charges. The mastery of Beryl Markham's horsemanship is the capacity that gives the flight and exploration of *West with the Night* its resonance. Hemingway's curious lack of interest in the horse, his insouciance at the goring of the picadors' horses and the replacement of their bowels with sawdust that they may continue the job cause me to wonder at him anew. Perhaps, he might have taken a lesson from Faulkner, who kept a few apples in his old coat for his horses and mules.

Indeed, to go forth with an animal, a dowager with her poodle, a hunter with his setter, a falconer with his hawk, a pirate with his parrot, is to enlarge one's affect such that the whole is greater than the sum of its parts. Poor horsemanship consists in suggesting that man and horse are separate. A horseman afoot is a wingless, broken thing, tyrannized by gravity. I have often been astounded after a great performance by horse and rider to encounter the rider afterward, a crumpled figure, negligible in every discernible way, a defeated, aging little man; or a crone, where moments ago a demon or a fire queen filled us with obsessive attention. And even the horses are turned into weary pensioners as, with empty saddles and lowered heads, they are led to their stalls to rest. For that burst of poetry, horse and rider have one another to thank.

Men's achievements have been enlarged by horses almost as if the animals' plangent silence implied what could never be merely said. Napoleon's famous horse Marengo, George Washington's gray Arab Magnolia, Grant's horse Cincinnati, Lee's horse Traveller, and Comanche, the one horse to survive the Battle of the Little Big Horn, were regarded with awe because horses, even the bones of horses, remember everything. Nothing focused the nation's mourning like the riderless black horse in the funeral cortege of John Kennedy.

At the Battle of Waterloo, men formed squares into which the wounded were brought for medical care. At the height of the battle, in the madness of the cannonading and death, the riderless horses of the cavalry, the caisson horses of the slaughtered gun crews attempted to penetrate the squares to be saved by the humans. And in the First World War, men subjected to unparalleled mayhem were stricken more by the plight of the horses than anything else. There is a special grief for the innocent caught up in mankind's murderous follies. The idea of horses with their self-absorbed innocence imbroiled in war is deeply disquieting. In Andrei Makine's memoir of Siberian life, *Dreams of My Russian Summers*, images of riderless but completely equipped White Russian cavalry horses, some with sabers swinging from the points at which they were plunged, running wild through a depopulated landscape suggest the fury of human conflict that has surpassed human control.

Hunting on horseback, following bird dogs through an oak forest, which I have done with indescribable pleasure and a hint of self-satisfaction perhaps at the very picture I imagined myself conveying, seems a coherent activity in which man and horse and dogs, birds and forest coalesce into something of duration. Add one motor scooter to this picture, or even the man trotting along on his inadequate legs, and you get something much reduced and thoroughly unbeautiful. From the time of the Greeks and, unrecorded, certainly before, it has been an explicit matter that mankind must have beauty to live.

2
ROPING, FROM
A to B

Over the years, I've had some failures of communication with different horses. I've been kicked, stepped on, and bitten. Bitten I liked least. My most trustworthy saddle horse leaned over once while I was cinching him up and clamped down on my upper leg, turning the thigh into what looked like a Central American sunset. I threw him down on the ground, half-hitched his feet together, and put a tarp over him. I let him up two hours later; he thought I was the greatest man in the world, one he wouldn't think of biting. Horses only remember the end of the story.

I bought a saddle horse named Cayenne who is supposed to go back to Yellow Jacket; and I used him for everyday riding, knocking around, going into the hills, checking ditches and head gates. He was a big easy-keeping sorrel with a blaze on his face—above all, a sensible horse.

He really taught me the ordinary aspects of a using horse: how their feet move in the rocks, when they're winded, how much water they need when they're hot, how you shouldn't let them eat when you're gathering cattle or they learn to dive at a gallop when idle hunger has struck; why you should get down when your lariat is caught under your horse's tail, why nose flies make them throw their heads in your face, why geldings make that noise at a trot, why even a good horse is liable to walk off and leave you; how a horse will, eventually, sell out for grain, how a horse can get you home from the mountains in the dark when a mule can't; and above all how, when you do such things long enough with one horse, you begin to see things in him, emotional things, even spiritual things.

Once when I was trimming Cayenne's feet, I thought he was leaning his weight on me and I thumped him with the rasp. He wouldn't eat for the rest of the day. The rasp certainly didn't hurt him. Now that I think of it, I offered him oats and he never sold out. There was a specific deal between that horse and me; and I had violated it. I never did it again. There was no question that I had hurt his feelings. A few weeks later, Cayenne made a cheap postcard of my thigh when I went to cinch him up.

You could rope a little bit off this horse. He was better than I was, anyway. He wouldn't jump out from under a rope and he'd let you heel calves. But you couldn't go to contests on him. He didn't like blasting out of the box with his ears pinned. He would jog up to a bunch of calves and let you snake them to the ground crew. You could turn him out for the winter and wrangle him in the spring and he'd be solid. I never had a vet bill on him.

The very little roping I did before I took up steer roping was what they called doctor roping and had to do with dabbing a loop on a cow's head to immobilize her long enough to provide medical aid. In addition to a rope, a lot of cowboys carry a plastic gun in the saddle for sending pills down troubled gullets, no six-shooter. Doctor roping is also done for calves with the scours, and these little brutes are "heeled"; their back feet are roped and they are skidded to the branding fire. Dehorned, branded, castrated, vaccinated, they are turned loose to return to their mothers. Most people nowadays use a chute and turn the calf on a table to do those things to him. But some ranches don't have a table and they need someone willing to heel calves all day long until lather collects around the latigo and cinch dees and linear rope burns form up and down the back of his hand from dallying.

"Dally" comes from the Mexican *dar la vuelta*— meaning to take a turn, a wrap around the saddle horn with the lariat to stop the creature in question, out there on the end of the rope, in the loop. Similarly, the rope that the Spanish hackamore horsemen wound and tied into reins and lead rope, the *mecate*, becomes, by the time it gets here to Montana, the "McCarthy."

When I first roped, I didn't know anything about dallying. It was hard and fast, the rope tied to the saddle horn. That's how contest calf ropers rope. They have to: they jump down and flank or leg the little cow and tie three legs with the pigging string, then throw their hands in the air. I don't like to get down and run all over the place like that. I'm getting too brittle. I like to stay mounted. Single steer trippers also rope hard and fast, but dally roping is an ancient craft still understood by a large number of people, handed down from the days of the old-time vaqueros, the Mexicans and Californios, who, with their hair-trigger spade-bit horses and braided riatas, were the best hands in the American West. The vaqueros and their horses are dead and gone; but something remains: hackamore reinsmen and dally ropers.

Contest roping was in the air. Many of my friends living on ranches, and some from nearby towns, started practicing during the week and competing, however inadequately, on the weekends.

Now, here's the way a dally-roping competition works: The steer chute is in the middle. Facing the chute to the right is the header's box and to the left is the heeler's box. I'm making a long story short. The header nods for the steer. The gate opens and the steer burns down the arena. The header ropes him and ducks off after dallying; he should "bump" the steer, that is, skid a foot or so of his rope on the saddle horn so that the steer isn't jerked into bucking, becoming a more difficult target for the heeler. The heeler ducks in with the steer just behind him, throws his trap, ropes the back feet, dallies, and stops the horse. The header turns to face the steer and the team is flagged for time, the steer stretched out.

It's hard for the header because everything is moving so fast. It's hard for the heading horse because he has to duck off with the steer, leaning into five hundred or six hundred hurtling pounds. It's hard for the heeler because those flying feet are hard to catch. It's hard for a heeling horse because he has to do that free-form crack-the-whip with the steer when the header sets him, then stop the steer and the head horse after the heeler has thrown his trick. That can be close to a ton hitting the end of thirty-five feet of seven-sixteenths-inch nylon rope.

Roping six-hundred-pound Corriente steers—Mexican horned cattle—without tying the end of the rope to the horn was not something that came to me quickly. For the longest time, it seemed less than sensible. But with repetition, the interior logic of its mechanics won out and I began to think not just in terms of getting the job done but of being a bit smoother in doing it.

There came a day when I couldn't find the saddle horn when I went to dally and broke my thumb in a few places, tearing the end off it. When I went to the emergency room, the nurse said, "Miss your dally?" "Tell the doctor I hate pain," I said. Nevertheless, he pulled my thumbnail out with a pair of needle-nosed pliers and told me I would have lost it anyway. Somehow, dally roping with that crazily loose-ended lariat, relying on wrapping the rope around the saddle horn to stop heavy running cattle, produced for me a kind of enchantment. And for at least a year, getting my wraps was always a close call.

Getting your wraps right is only half the story. There is, of course, the matter of your horse. If he's a good horse, he hits wide open on his second stride out of the box. Everything is moving. Staying loose and not tensing up is the roper's biggest obstacle. My own mental drill is based on advice from a fine old roper: "Remember one thing when you back your horse into the box. There are nine hundred million Chinese who don't care whether you catch the steer or not." This helps; though, in the heat of a big roping, it's hard to picture those indifferent Chinese. Everything is easier if your horse is more levelheaded than you are, if he backs his butt into the corner of the box to better watch the gate and coolly waits for his steer.

This same roper told me another wonderful thing: "Don't pitch your rope like you were through with it."

When you first catch a steer you halfway wish you were through with it; the steer is hauling ass and that hard nylon rope heats to seeming incandescence when you run about eighteen inches of it through your hand. You have to run it a little; the steer is moving away and you need to let it slip as you start down to dally. Fundamentally, you should know how to run the whole rope and let it go, if you have to, without getting a turn around your hand. It's easy to lose a finger roping and almost as easy to lose a hand as a finger.

Montanans kicked their horses out into the hills in the 1920s, with the advent of the automobile. After the Second World War, they went up and caught them again. These days, Hondas and Ski-Doos are pressing the stock horse once again. You can get a bit of pressure now for having horses at all, from people who consider them an affectation or a waste of money. But a lot of the old boys are still around, hard-bitten romantics with Red Man coming out of the corners of their mouths who want to be "plumb mounted" on some shining pony that goes back to studs like Old Sorrel or Oklahoma Star or Joe Hancock or My Texas Dandy or Midnight or Zantanon ("the Mexican Man o' War"). For years, we stood an old foundation-bred stallion, King Benjiman, on our ranch. I bought him on impulse and at a thrilling discount based on his owner's imminent departure for a federal correctional facility in Oklahoma. It was surprising how many old ranchers and cowboys brought us their mares to breed to a horse whose genetics are barely remembered today.

Many of these same people turned up at the jackpot ropings I frequented, as a contributor at first, and then as an occasional winner. These were ranch hands, itinerants, old nighthawks from big outfits, some with nothing but their skills and prospects of unemployment, who nevertheless were always on the lookout for something they could do for fun. They turned up at one or another of the many remote roping arenas, homemade out of planks and railroad ties. Some of these ropers were born on ranches and are now boilermakers on the Amtrak or surveyors on I-90, shooting in four-lanes. Some grew up in local towns or, perhaps, Indiana. But they had in common a love of some good pony, maybe living on baled hay out behind the IGA store, and that hard rope they were forever handling.

Out of places with better weather, but mostly California, where dally roping is oldest, there came a lot of new ropers, some of them hauling horses behind weird hot rigs; professionals, rope hustlers, cowboys from Sheridan, Wyoming, in their twenties wearing King Rope hats, caps promoting Camarillo Ropers' Products, Powder River portable corrals, the L.A. Dodgers; and down in the pens beneath a streaky western sky, a kid would be moving Corriente steers toward the chute in a T-shirt that advertised a heavy-metal band. You could tell these new ropers by their aggressive style, too, standing straight up in the stir-rups, holding their reins and coils down close to the horse's neck, sitting only when they dallied. And they often ran well-schooled horses that didn't look abused, horses they had broken themselves.

One atavism in rural roping, and maybe it's every-where, is the business of hexing other ropers, making signs against the competition in the dirt, writing the name of the enemy on ceremonial mounds, and the general directing of black-magic signs and sema-phores as well as jinxing, spitting, upside-down crosses, and the evil eye aimed at horse, rider, or the saddle horn. One arena owner said, "I don't believe none of that stuff. I do throw fellows out for hexing other ropers because it seems to upset folks." At most of the ropings I go to everybody looks so nor-mal—ropers, trailers, horses, families, six-packs of Great Falls in the cooler. It's always a shock to find Dad behind the pens with his partner, drawing hexes in the dust.

Anyway, my boy now owned Cayenne and I was looking for a heel horse. I finally found one, named Dan, and I bought him: sixteen hands, buckskin geld-ing, 1,220 pounds; by a quarter-horse stud out of a thoroughbred mare. I liked him because he was big and still catty. He reined well, got into the ground on his stops with everything he had when you asked him, and was, in general, a horse who liked to hunt cattle. Also, he didn't pack his head so high I couldn't see where I was roping. He was a hard-knocking horse in every respect and his eight years had given him a lot of contusions: splints on his front legs, bursitis, and a navicular fracture. He had to be specially shod in front, bars across the bases to control heel expansion, rolled toes, and set at exactly fifty-four degrees. He had spent years gathering bucking horses in the hills. He was a horse who never, ever blew his cool, even to standing like a rock when he got gored in the shoulder or when a wild steer wrapped his legs with hard nylon. Once when a steer flipped in front of him, he vaulted the steer and in three circling jumps had me back in position to rope.

I was at a jackpot roping, sitting on Dan. A dog went by, a sore leg carried in the air. A roper walked along behind, doing little reverse whirls and tricks with his lariat; looked at the dog, then me.

"I call that dog Arithmetic."

"?"

"Because he puts down three and carries one."

Over at the stock scale, I had just lost a dollar betting on the weight of my own horse. "I don't seem to have a gift for this," I said, walking off.

"Same dog bit me," said the roper with the three-legged dog. Dogs in the air. One was in the heading box on the fourth go-round and had to be carried out like a baby, four feet in the air, looking sheepishly into the stands.

It was an eight-steer roping. We had a steer kick out on the seventh; then my header broke the barrier and we lost sixty bucks.

He said, "That was quick."

We'd been roping all day and the horses were steaming. There was no change at the concession stand and the coffee was gone. It was dark and the general call for a grudge match, "One steer for a fast go," was ignored. The dog guy walked past and said, "I could use some goddamned day-money. I live clear to Miles City."

I had a nice rope burn from where my horn wrap had slipped. I loaded my horse and went to the Emigrant Saloon. I drank three "depth charges" with a bunch of ropers at the bar and played all the Jimmy Buffett as well as a couple of songs a couple of girls said had been written for them. After depth charge number three I had a wave of affection for my horse. I went out to the trailer and opened the little door and looked into one of his great eyes.

"Hello, Dan," I said and went home happy.

That June, I bought ten Corriente steers. They had wintered in Mexico and were gaunt and wild, fast desert cattle with horns carried high on their heads like antlers. I turned them out in a small pasture across from the house, maybe twenty acres, to put on some weight; and they vanished. I thought they had jumped the cattle guard. But when I rode across, I began to spot them, every once in a while, popping up out of brush that couldn't hide a cat. They were completely wild cattle, could live on anything, thrifty.

They were also what is called breachy; a fence meant almost nothing to them. And so I was always driving one down from a neighboring ranch. They were the UFOs of my area, with those antlers, fabulous speed, and an uncanny ability to disappear. I thought they were fascinating but I heard from time to time that my neighbors were sick of seeing them on their places.

As we got to know them, we named many of them: Old Blue for his color, Crazy because he gored the horse the first time he was roped, Al Capone for his rugged Americanism, and A-2-Gas for his blaze of early speed.

Al Capone earned his stripes the day he took a hard right through the plank sides of the arena. Then he went through some fences and moved into the deep grass of a nearby ranch. When we went to get him, we planned an attack very carefully because there was no telling where he'd stop if we got him running again.

Steadily, we advanced: me; Allen Ray Carter, my roping partner; his brother, Little C.; and Paul Lyman, who used to ride broncs on the West Coast. We felt we had this handled.

We approached in deep grass that swept our stirrups. It was evening and the individual peaks of the Gallatins were propped against their shadows. Somewhere ahead of us, we knew, Al Capone listened for our minatory footfalls, ready and willing to fool with our expectations.

The wind swept the grass down. We saw the black tips of Al Capone's horns moving in precise abrupt arcs. Our plan was to move in with steady and unexcited progress; at the last minute, Little C. would race in and fire a head loop, one of us would back him up, and Al Capone would go home in a trailer.

As we moved in, the rotary movements of Capone's horns grew more intent. We got incredibly close. It was time. Little C. spurred his horse forward and Capone vaulted from the grass. Little C.'s loop snaked out and caught the horns.

But Little C. missed his dally and Al Capone was burning to the east, trailing a twenty-dollar heading rope. Allen Ray overtook him once on his big buckskin, roped him, and missed his dally, too. Capone was eating into our outfit.

When he reached Route 89, he broke the fences on both sides of the highway, trailing wire and sixty feet of three-eighths-inch nylon, not to mention lathered horses and riders whose irrational babbling increased with every rod of gopher-riddled ground.

Capone hit the upper Yellowstone River and turned right. Things were beginning to tell. He merely dog-trotted past the dining room window of the last ranch we passed. And no one seemed to be sure whether or not he had his heart in it when he dove into the fish pond. In any case, he made an easy target for ropers, with nothing but horns and nostrils above the surface as he dog-paddled through the aquatic weeds. We took him home and named him. The horses were spent; and we've all been a little proud of that steer ever since. He's now in a big band of roping cattle and when, at a jackpot, we see him in the chute, banging his horns against the steel just to be mean, we glance at each other and one of us says that revered name: *Al Capone.*

At the Gardiner, Montana, rodeo I had a number of reasons to be nervous. It was a one-steer roping, no average. We were roping Sunday after all of Saturday's ropers and the entry fee was high. My partner, Allen Ray Carter, was thinking about that entry fee. His wife was about to have a baby (a boy, Gene, now out of college), and there was some feeling that paying out sixty bucks was a real instance of pounding sand down a rat hole.

Then, when we were unloading our horses, two of the state's best ropers came by and the heeler said, "We're going to take your money." It didn't seem impossible. My girl was up from Alabama (we've been married over twenty years now) and she always covered her face when I went into the box with those nine hundred million Chinese.

My son sat on the rail and took a perspective of clarity only a ten-year-old has for his father. "You can beat those assholes, Dad." Now that he's in his thirties and has his own son, he has cleaned up his language.

"Don't say 'assholes,' Tom."

"Ropers." From an early age, he took a dim view of my rodeo foolishness.

"I like my fingers, Dad. Look at your hand."

I looked at my hand, crooked thumb, rope burns, enlarged knuckles, and I felt good because I'd been afraid that, as a writer, I would always have these Ivory Snow hands; and, in fact, some cur had once said I had writer's hands, which really got to me, as I am someone who wants to be a rugged guy in the West and not some horrid nancy with pink palms. (Take note, arty types out there in the Rocky Mountains: roping is a good fast way to acquire local-color hands.) At the same time, you don't want to be the one roper they call Flipper. Or worse: a header up north overran a steer, threw his horse, burst his spleen, and died, turning colors as he staggered after his steer dragging a lariat. He'd just sold his ranch to have more time to rope. There's no need of going that far.

That day in Gardiner, nobody wanted me to come out of the box and just be a writer about it. Nor did I, if I could help it. I wanted Allen Ray to turn that steer like lightning so I could doublehock him and stop the clock.

I went down where the doggers started to go, to check out the cattle. It was the end of the summer and the steers were big and sour. They were setting up and the doggers were having to just kind of get down and shock them before the steers had a chance to set back and knock out their teeth. I noticed the hazers seemed to be trying to squeeze the cattle right up against the dogging horses. And, in general, there were numerous signs that these were indeed sour cattle.

When we entered, they told us we had to wear long-sleeved shirts and cowboy hats. One of the younger toughs said, "I always rope in tank tops and Hush Puppies."

"Not here you don't," said the man.

Finally, they announced the team that was up, the team that was on deck, and the team in the hole. When you get to the point where your name is on the loudspeaker, it's time to warm up the horse, forget the prickling palms, build and unbuild your loop, and pick your way horseback through the kids from the concession stand.

Then they called us. Someone swung open the big gate and we rode into the arena. At this point a cloud forms around you and you can't see anything but your steer.

I built my loop and rode into the box, swung Dan toward the steer, and backed him into the corner. Allen Ray rode in on the other side and I was thinking, Let this be an honest hard-running steer, and let me be winding up and standing in my stirrups when we clear the box. Girlfriends, children, expectant mothers, all seemed to require we catch our steer.

Allen Ray looked over and I nodded that I was ready. Dan was pricking alternate ears waiting for the chute to bang.

Allen Ray reined his horse to look at the steer, and nodded.

The gate slammed open and the steer was running. Dan came on so hard I had to keep my left hand on the horn, gradually coming up in the stirrups against that acceleration. I hazed the steer in close to Allen Ray until his loop went out and I faded a little to make that corner when he set the steer.

The steer tried to fall, but Allen Ray spurred his horse to line him out. Dan swerved in and I pitched my loop, caught both hind feet, and dallied. I felt Dan suck down under me, and the steer stretched out as the flag went down.

We won.

When we released the steer I galloped up the rail. I don't win that often. My son was smiling like the first sunrise, and when I rode by he said, "Hey, Dad!" just to show everybody we knew each other.

Then someone offered to buy a victory drink at the Two Bit Saloon. Everybody headed for town and I loaded my horse, stowed my saddle, and my girl and I piled into the truck ready for a celebration.

The truck wouldn't start. Probably something about the motor. That wasn't an area of interest for me.

3
BUSTER

Almost a decade ago, I was working in what is ponderously known as the motion picture industry, which required my presence for a long spell in Los Angeles. I spent my time in script conferences with a movie star who managed to wake up in a different world each day. Sometimes our story took place high in the mountains; other times the scene moved to the desert or to a nonexistent little town that derived its features from the star's days in movie houses, when he dreamed of working on his draw instead of on his lines. Some days the Indians won, some days the law. This was about to be one of the last cowboy movies America would put up with.

But myth was something I was still interested in. And so, in the evenings, my wife and I would drive out to Chino, where our friend Joe Heim trained cutting horses. We worked cattle under the lights, an absolute anomaly in a run-down suburb. His place was very small, a couple of acres maybe, and the horses and cows were penned wherever space could be found. I particularly remember an old oak tree where we used to hang the big festoon of bridles and martingales. Joe lived in a trailer house, did his books on a desk at one end and slept in the other. On those warm nights when cattle and horses did things that required decoding, Joe would always begin, "What Buster would do here is . . . " I had never seen Buster Welch, but his attempts to understand an ideal relationship between horsemen and cattle sent ripples anywhere that cows grazed, from Alberta to the Mexican border. It would be many years before I drove into his yard in West Texas.

Buster Welch was born and more or less raised north of Sterling City, Texas, on the divide between the Concho and Colorado rivers. His mother died shortly after he was born, and he was brought up by his grandfather, a retired peace officer, and his grandmother on a stock farm in modest self-sufficiency. Buster came from a line of people who had been in Texas since before the Civil War, Tennesseans by origin. Growing up in the Roosevelt years in a part of Texas peculiarly isolated from modern times, Buster was ideally situated to understand and convey the practices of the cowboys of an earlier age to an era rapidly leaving its own mythology. The cutting horse is a sacred link to those times, and its use and performance are closer to the Japanese martial theater than to rodeo. Originally, a cutting horse was used to separate individual cattle for branding or doctoring. From the "brag" horses of those early days has evolved the cutting horse, which refines the principles of stock handling and horsemanship for the purposes of competition.

When Buster was a young boy, his father remarried and moved his wife, her two children, and Buster to Midland and worked as a tank boss for Atlantic Richfield. Buster's separation from Sterling City and his grandparents and their own linkage to the glorious past had the net result of turning Buster into a truant from the small, poor school he attended, a boy whose dreams were triggered by the herds of cattle that were trailed past the schoolhouse to the stockyards. He became a youthful bronc buster at the stockyards and was befriended by people like Claude "Big Boy" Whatley, a man so strong he could catch a horse by the tail, take hold of a post, and instruct Buster to let the other horses out of the corral. By the time Buster reached the sixth grade, he had run away a number of times, and at thirteen he ran away for keeps. In making his departure on a cold night, he led a foul old horse named Handsome Harry well away from the house so his family wouldn't hear the horse bawling when it bucked. He climbed on the horse and rode away. From there he went to work for Foy and

Leonard Proctor, upright and industrious cowmen who handled as many as thirty thousand head of cattle a year. Buster began by breaking broncs, grubbing prickly pear, chopping firewood, wrangling horses, and holding the cut when a big herd was being worked, a lowly job where much can be learned.

When you see Buster's old-time herd work under the lights in Will Rogers coliseum or at the Astrodome in Houston, that is where it began. The Proctors are still alive, revered men in their nineties, descendants of trail drovers and Indian fighters. From them, Buster learned to shape large herds of cattle and began the perfection of his minimalist style of cutting horsemanship and cattle ranching in general. He worked with horses that "weren't the kind a man liked to get on." But in those early days, he was around some horses that "went on," including Jesse James, who became the world champion cutting horse. Nevertheless, he probably spent more time applying 62 Smear, a chloroform-based screwworm concoction, to afflicted cattle than to anything more obviously bound for glory.

Buster rode the rough string for the storied Four Sixes Ranch at and around Guthrie. One of the horses had been through the bronc pen two or three times and was so unrepentant that you had to ride him all day after you topped him off in the morning, relieving yourself down the horse's shoulder rather than getting off, and at the end of the day, buck down to the end of the reins, turn around, and scare the horse back before he could paw and strike you. But this was an opportunity to be around those good and important cowmen and to work cattle out with the chuck wagon or from the permanent camps on that big ranch. Buster is remembered for his white shirts and for being the only man able to ride the rough string and stay clean. Hands circulated from the Four Sixes to the Matador and the Pitchfork in what amounted to graduate schools for cowboys. Off and on in that period, Buster rode saddle broncs at the casual rodeos of the day, where the prospects for injury far outweighed the opportunity for remuneration. There was certainly in Buster's life a drive for individuality in his work that might have been realized earlier if someone had been good enough to leave him a ranch. Even by then ranches were in the hands of "sons, sons-in-law, and sons of bitches." To this day, he sees himself primarily as a rancher. But until recently, a cutting horse was an essential part of a rancher's life. Now it is quite possible for a cutting horse to never see open country; too many of them live the lives of caged birds, with an iron routine from box stall to training pen to hot walker to box stall, moving through the seasons of big-purse events to long retirement in breeding programs.

By the time Buster Welch began to establish himself as a horseman, beyond someone who could get the early saddlings on rough stock and bring a horse to some degree of finish and refinement, the cutting horse began to come into its own as a contest animal. The adversity of the Texas cattle business had a lot to do with Welch's career. His plan had always been to use his advantages in training the cutting horse to establish himself in the cow business. And he was well on his way to making that happen in the fifties, running eight hundred cows on leased land, when the drought struck. Ranches big and small, including some that had survived from the days of the frontier, vanished forever. It ruined many a stouter operator than Buster Welch. In those tough times a horse called Marion's Girl came into Buster's life. The weather focused his options, and the mare focused his talent. Buster went on the road with Marion's Girl and made her the world champion cutting horse that year, 1954. If he ever looked back, he never said so.

I spent one winter in the Deep South, working and going to weekend cuttings. I had been staying mainly in Alabama and by April was getting ready to go home to Montana. I had managed to catch a ride for my horses from Hernando, Mississippi, to Amarillo, where I wanted to make a cutting, then go on home. This all seemed ideal for paying a visit to Buster at Merkel en route.

Buster greeted me from the screen door of the bunkhouse. The ranch buildings were set among the steadily ascending hills that drew your mind forever outward into the distance. I began to understand how Buster has been able to refuel his imagination while the competition has burned out and fallen behind. There was a hum of purpose here. It was a horseman's experimental station right in the heart of the range cattle industry.

Buster and I rode the buckboard over the ranch, taking in Texas at this remote end of the Edwards Plateau. Was this the West? The South? The groves of oak trees and small springs, the sparse distribution of cattle on hillsides that seemed bountiful in a restrained sort of way, the deep wagon grooves in rock. We clattered through a dry wash in this Texas desert, where cactus and blue quail seem to belong and where one sensed that man's occupancy must be conducted delicately if it was to last.

"Nobody can ranch as cheap as I can," said Buster, leaning out over the team to scrutinize it for adjustment, the heavy latigo reins draped familiarly in his hands. "If I have to." But when we passed an old gouge in the ground, he stopped and said ruefully, "It took the old man that had this place first a lifetime to fill that trash hole up. We haul more than that away every week." Each year Buster and his wife, Sheila, win hundreds of thousands of dollars riding cutting horses but there was something about this prosperity with which he was uncomfortable.

Of the hands working on Buster's ranch, hailing from Texas, Washington, and Australia, there was an array of talent in general cow work. But so far as I could discern, nobody didn't want to be a cutting-horse trainer. There is considerable competition and activity for people interested in cutting horses in Australia, but the country is so vast, especially the cattle country, that well-educated hands go home and basically dry up for lack of seeing one another or for being unable to cope with the mileage necessary to get to cuttings. Nevertheless, such as the situation is, much of the talent in Australia grew up under Buster's tutelage. Buster is very fond of his Australians and thinks they are like the old-time Texans who took forever to fill the trash hole behind the house. Buster has said to me several times that he would like to have lived in Australia.

Cowboys have their well-known high spirits, but under Buster's guidance they are quiet and polite. At meals, they rise, introduce themselves, shake hands, and try to be helpful. In their limited spare time these cowboys make the Saturday night run to town, or they attend Bible classes, or they hole up in the bunkhouse to listen to heavy metal on their boom boxes. Buster finds something to like in each of them: one is industrious, another is handy with machinery, another has light hands with a colt, and so on. Every time he works his horse, they watch him studiously, reminding me of the advantages of apprenticeship: there was a sharp contrast between these vigilant young men and the barely awake denizens of a college lecture hall. Buster has been blessed by continuity and by an enormous pride in his heritage. One of his forebears rode with Fitzhugh Lee and, refusing to surrender when the Confederacy fell, was never heard from again; another fought to defend Vicksburg. Buster's grandfather was a sheriff in West Texas, still remembered with respect. There are a lot of pictures of his ancestors around the place, weathered, unsmiling Scotch-Irish faces. Buster doesn't smile for pictures either, though he spends a lot of time smiling or grinning at the idea of it all, the peculiar, delightful purposefulness of life and horses, the rightness of cattle and West Texas, but above all, the perfection and opportunity of today, the very day we have right here.

By poking around and prying among the help, I was able to determine that the orderly world I perceived as Buster's camp was something of an illusion and that there were many days that began quite unpredictably. In fact, there was the usual disarray of any artist's mise-en-scène, though we had here, instead of a squalid Parisian atelier, a cattle ranch. But I never questioned that this was an artist's place, one which moved more to inspiration than routine.

For example, the round pen. Buster invented its present use. Heretofore, cutting horses not trained on the open range—and those had become exceedingly rare—were trained in square arenas. Buster trained that way. But one day a song insistently went through his head, a song about "a string with no end," and Buster realized that that was what he was looking for, a place where the logic of a cow horse's motion and stops could go on in continuity as it once did on the open range, a place where walls and corners could never eat a horse and its rider and stop the flow. By moving from a square place of training to a circular one, Buster achieved a more accurate simulation of the range. A horse could be worked in a round place without getting mentally "burned" by tedious interruptions (corners); the same applied to the rider, and since horse and rider in cutting are almost the same thing, what applied to the goose applied to the gander. The round pen made the world of cutting better; even the cattle kept their vitality and inventiveness longer. But Buster's search for a place where the movement could be uninterrupted was something of a search for eternity, at least his eternity, which inevitably depends on a horseman tending stock. Just as the Plains Indians might memorialize the buffalo hunt in the beauty of their dancing, the rider on a cutting horse can celebrate the life of the open range forever.

Buster Welch's horses have a "look," and this matter of look, of style, is important. The National Cutting Horse Association book on judging cutting horses makes no mention of this; but it is a life-and-death factor. There are "plain" horses, or "vanilla" horses, and there are "good-moving" horses, or "scorpions." Interestingly enough, if categorization were necessary, Buster's horses tend to be plain. It is said that it takes a lot of cow to make one of his horses win a big cutting. On the other hand, his cutting horses are plain in the way that Shaker furniture is plain. They are so direct and purposeful that their eloquence of motion can be missed. Furthermore, we may be in the age of the baroque horse, the spectacular, motion-wasteful products of training pens and indoor arenas. Almost no one has the open range background of Buster Welch anymore.

Those who worked cattle for a long time on the open range learned a number of things about the motion of cow horses. A herd of cattle is a tremulous, explosive thing, as anxious to change shapes as a school of fish is. Control is a delicate matter. A horse that runs straight and stops straight doesn't scare cattle. And a straight-stopping horse won't fall with you either. Buster Welch's horses run straight and stop straight. They're heads-up, alert horses, unlikely to splay out on the floor of the arena and do something meretricious for the tourists. They are horses inspired by the job to be done and not by the ambitions of the rider. Buster has remarked that he would like to win the world championship without ever getting his horse out of a trot. That would make a bleak day for the Fort Worth Chamber of Commerce but a bright one for the connoisseur.

There were three or four people hanging around the bunkhouse when we got back from taking in the ranch. One was the daughter of a friend of mine in the Oklahoma panhandle, there with her new husband. They had all just been to a horse sale in Abilene, where they ran some young horses through. They were in shock. They just sprawled out on the benches in the dogtrot, which was a kind of breezeway, and took in what a rude surprise the price of horses had gotten to be. "Look at it this way," said Buster. "You don't have to feed those suckers anymore." He looked around at the faces. "You are the winners," he added for emphasis. There was no reaction from the "winners."

Buster is practical. He helped start the futurity for three-year-old horses because the good, broke, open horses lasted so long; the need for trainers was small and even shrinking. He thought it might be good to steal a notion from the automobile industry and build some planned obsolescence into the western cow horse. He may have underestimated our hunger for novelty.

The boom in cutting, the millions in prize money given away annually, is largely spent on the young horses, especially three- and four-year-olds. Syndicates have proliferated, and certified public accountants lead shareholders past the stalls of the assets. This year's horses spring up and vanish like Cabbage Patch dolls, and the down-the-road open horse is in danger of becoming a thing of the past, an object of salvage. If the finished open horse doesn't regain its former stature, the ironic effect of large purses for young horses and the concentration of those events in Texas will be to deprive cutting of its national character and to consign it to the minor leagues.

One of the best horses Buster ever trained is a stud named Haida's Little Pep. When Buster asked me if there was any horse in particular I wanted to ride, I said Haida's Little Pep. Buster sent a stock trailer over to Sterling City, where the horse was consorting with seventy mostly accepting mares. I couldn't wait to see the horse whose desire and ability, it had been said, had forced Buster to change his training methods. (He actually leaks some of these rumors himself.) Buster watched the men unload the stallion, in his characteristic stance: elbows back, hands slightly clenched, like a man preparing to jump into a swimming pool. Haida's Little Pep stepped from the trailer and gazed coolly around at us, a thickset sorrel stud with a demeanor of quiet confidence.

We saddled him and went into the arena. "Go ahead and cut you a cow," said Buster. Two cowboys held a small herd of cattle at one end. My thought was, What? No last-minute instructions?

I climbed aboard. Here I had a different view of this famous beast: muscle, compact horse muscle; in particular a powerful neck that developed from behind the ears, expanding back toward the saddle to disappear between my knees. The stud stood awaiting some request from me. I didn't know if, when I touched him with a spur, he was going to squeal and run through the cedar walls of the pen or just hump his back, put his head between his legs, and send me back to Montana. But he just moved off, broke but not broke to death; the cues seemed to mean enough to get him where you were going but with none of the death-defying spins of the ride-'em-and-slide-'em school. Haida's Little Pep, thus far, felt like a mannerly ranch horse. I headed for the herd.

Once among the cattle, I had a pleasant sensation of the horse moving as requested but not bobbing around trying to pick cattle himself. His deferring to me made me wonder if he was really cooperating in this enterprise at all. As I sorted a last individual, he stood so flat-footed and quiet that I asked myself if he had mentally returned from the stallion station. I put the reins down. The crossbred steer gazed back at the herd, and when he turned to look at us, Haida's Little Pep sank slowly on his hocks. When the steer bolted, the horse moved at a speed slightly more rapid than the ability of cattle to think and in four turns removed the steer's willpower and stopped him.

The horse's movements were hard and sudden but so unwasteful and accurate that he was easy to ride. Because of the way this horse was broke, I began thinking about the problems of working these cattle. I immediately sensed that the horse and I had the same purpose. I've been on many other horses that produced no such feeling. There was too much discrepancy between our intentions. We wanted to cut different cattle. They didn't want to hold and handle cattle; they wanted to chase them. They didn't want to stop straight; they wanted to round their turns and throw me onto the saddle horn. But this high-powered little stud was correct, flat natural, well intentioned, and extremely easy to ride.

We looked at some old films in Buster's living room. They were of Marion's Girl, whom Buster had trained in the fifties, the mare who had done a lot to change the rest of his life. I had long heard about her, but I remember Buster describing her to me for the first time at a cutting on Sweet Grass Creek in Montana. The ranch there was surrounded by a tall, steep bluff covered with bunchgrass and prickly pear; it was maybe a thousand feet high and came down to the floor of the valley at a steep angle. Buster had said that Marion's Girl would run straight down something like that to head a cow, stop on her rear end, and slide halfway to the bottom before turning around to drive the cow. As all great trainers feel about all great horses, Buster felt that Marion's Girl had trained him; more explicitly, she had trained him to train the modern cutting horse. At that time most cutting horses kind of ran sideways and never stopped quite straight. Buster considered that to be a degraded period during which the proper practices of the open range were forgotten. Marion's Girl, like some avatar from the past, ran hard, stopped straight, and turned through herself without losing ground to cattle.

As I watched the old film, I could see this energetic and passionate mare working in what looked like an old corral. Though she has been dead for many years, the essence of the modern cow horse was there, move after move. In the film Buster looked like a youngster, but he bustled familiarly around with his elbows cocked, ready to dive into the pool.

"Are horses smart or dumb?" I asked Buster.

"They are very smart," he said with conviction. "Very intelligent. And if you ask one to do something he was going to do anyway, you hurt his feelings, you insult his intelligence."

Everyone wants to know what Buster Welch's secret in training horses is; and that's it. Only it's not a secret. All you need to know is what the horse was going to do anyway. But to understand that, it may be necessary to go back forty years and sit next to your bedroll in front of the Scharbauer Hotel in Midland, waiting for some cowman to come pick you up. If you got a day's work, it might be on a horse that would just love to kill you. It was a far cry from the National Cutting Horse Association Futurity, but it was the sort of thing Buster began with, and it lies at the origins of his education as to what horses are going to do anyway.

I stayed in the living room to talk to Sheila Welch while, outside the picture window, horses warmed up in the cedar pen. Sheila is a cool beauty, a fine-boned blonde from Wolf Point, Montana, and a leading interpreter, through her refined horsemanship, of Buster's training. She is capable of looking better on Buster's horses than he does and certainly could train a horse herself. Cutting horses move hard and fast enough to make rag dolls of ordinary horsemen, but Sheila goes beyond poise to a kind of serenity. A little bit later, Sheila stood in the pen waiting for someone to give her the big sorrel horse she has used to dispirit the competition for years. When he was brought up, she slipped up into the saddle, eased into the herd, and imperceptibly isolated a single cow in front of her. The horse worked the cow with the signature speed and hard stops; Sheila seemed to float along cooperatively and forcefully at once. But I noticed that in the stops, those places where it is instinctive to grip with one's leg and where it is preferable not to touch the horse at all, there was a vague jingling sound. What was that vague jingling sound? It was the sound of iron stirrups rattling on Sheila's boots.

At its best, the poetry of the open range remains, not in the scared, melodramatic antics of the stunt horses but in the precision of that minority singled out as "cow horses," sometimes lost in the artificial atmosphere of the big events.

For years, I have tried to understand Buster's way of training horses. In the age of proliferating horse whisperers, his methods are direct, based on reaching an understanding with the horse that there is a job to be done. In this sense, he is not seeking companionship with horses, though his relationship with horses he likes, such as his all-around using horse Enchilada, is equivalent to the consistent respect one accords an esteemed co-worker. In the beginning of training a cow horse, the horseman knows the job and the horse does not. Therefore, a progression of steps toward wider understanding is devised: trailing a cow, driving a cow, anticipating a cow, and so on. This part can be fairly easily understood by one undertaking the training of a cow horse. Less easy is knowing horses well enough to know the rate at which the horse can absorb the learning, and knowing when the learning has stuck sufficiently that interdependent further steps may be taken. Timing is also critical; one is inclined to say that it is everything, except that some trainers with good principles, good consistency, good work habits, and good understanding of the horse get along quite well with merely adequate timing. That is, their sense of timing is sufficient to take the horse to the level at which the trainer may gracefully retire from suggestion making and let the horse's own timing rise to the fore. This is known as "getting out of the way" or, more to the point, "letting the cow train the horse." Once this stage has been reached, the most important issue is riding the horse correctly. I once gave Eugen Herrigel's little masterpiece *Zen in the Art of Archery* to Buster to read and he concluded that its application to horsemanship was that if you are thinking about your riding you are interfering with your horse.

Interfering with your horse. Therein lies the core of respect Buster Welch has for horses. A rider may train a horse to understand the basic parameters of cow work but then the opportunity must exist for the horse to make his contribution. The great Canadian trainer Dave MacGregor told me that years ago when they would drive four- and five-year-old wild horses from the open range in Alberta into the corral where they were to be trained, these unbroke horses ran full tilt and made long sliding, straight stops of the kind trainers tear their hair out trying to produce in their mounts. His point, like Buster's, is that a horse can already do many of the things we require of it, if we would just get out of the way and let them do it. Avoiding this redundancy is at the heart of Buster's training. Therefore, when a horse is working as he should, it is essential that the rider take a light and relaxed seat in the saddle, with a rein hand that is assuredly down on the horse's neck and with eyes focused on the same thing the horse is watching, the cow. If no training is required, the rider's body, in Buster's words, "should have no opinion." If it becomes necessary to "call on" the horse, that is, ask him to do something more, the rider shouldn't overspecify the request by special leg pressure or fancy spurring but merely "knock" the horse, a kind of reminder in the form of a light kick, which instead of offering specific instruction to the horse honors the horse by saying, "Come on, you know what I'm talking about." These sorts of communications in which the horse is treated as knowing a great deal about the job to be done have the result of leaving the brightness and originality of the horse, its indelible spirit and vigor, there for all to see, rather than that spectacle of obedience, of compliance, in an animal that is all too trained. Buster has isolated the irreducible basics of cow work, the straight run, the hard stop, "rating," or the quick estimation of the cow's speed, and made them the ABC's of training. Within these requirements, the horse may indulge the intricacies of his own ideas of how things are to be done. It is here that we see with delight how different one horse is from another.

I am sometimes concerned that the kind of cutting horse that Buster Welch advocates is becoming a thing of the past but there are enough good hands who feel as I do that the day may be long in coming. I recall watching a spectacular horse at the Augusta Futurity, a real crowd pleaser, who sat way down onto the root of his tail getting turned, or spun around, in effect overreacting to the cow, whose danger to him was greatly emphasized by much spurring. Buster watched bemusedly and said, "I don't know any situation, indoors or out, where that is a good way to handle a cow." Yet, it was a winning look. Later, we watched Miss Silver Pistol at a cutting in Amarillo. Here again was a belly crawling, over-revved, thoroughly passionate horse, one of the great winners of modern times. I sat watching with an Englishman, a literary man, who had never seen a cow horse before and had just watched about a hundred of them; yet, he was startled into attention by this mare. Buster commented, "This cuttin's gettin' to be more and more like professional wrestling but *damn* that Miss Silver Pistol can moan and pound the mat!" He has stated that today's horses break so far in heading a cow that you wonder if the cow will ever *catch* the horse.

There is a kind of sweet spot on a cow when you are running across the ground trying to hold her. You basically try to keep the nose of your horse at the juncture of the cow's neck and shoulder. This generally, in a stride or two, will turn the cow. Of course it can transpire at blazing speed. In the classic style, the horse, through swiftness, quick stops, and general agility, maintains this position. A riskier and more spectacular way of stopping a cow is by simply heading it; that is, driving the horse far enough past the cow that the cow turns to go the other way. This results in broader and more extreme movements, left and right, in stopping the cow. Stopping cattle as close to immediately as possible is the contemporary style. Since cattle are unpredictable this style often results in the abandoned, crowd-pleasing runs that win today's cuttings. "To win," says one top modern trainer, "your horse needs to be ginnin' around." Buster's dream of winning the world without getting his horse out of a trot does not fit this approach.

In the modern method, a horse does not simply rate and stop with a cow. After the cow and horse have stopped, the trainer may "take the horse across" the cow, bringing the horse to a position whereby it faces in the opposite direction of the cow, then returning the horse to the center of the cow. As this becomes muscle memory, a horse runs and stops with the cow, then immediately jumps up into the middle of the cow. Instead of a neat and finished movement, one is presented with a quick, synchronized double motion that suggests that the job of the cutting horse is not so much to control the cow but to challenge it. When properly accomplished it is a glorious thing to observe, attesting to heightened athleticism and a kind of glittering commentary on the idea of cow work. Indeed, the creative side of a horse's nature may be more visible in this style, as it is considerably less restrained.

On the other hand, it is very far from the work of the ranch and while this latest version of the cutting horse is a delight to present to a judge on the cultivated footing of a modern arena, this same horse would be an absolute nightmare with which to work cattle on the open range. The rider, though moving few cattle to their objectives, would end the day with raw buttocks and an enhanced sense of futility. Without a sanctioned judge to reward him, he might feel that quieter sports beckoned.

In training horses, Buster's advantage is a broader base of knowledge from which to draw. He frequently starts out under a tree at daybreak with a cup of coffee, reading history, fiction, politics, anything that seems to expand his sense of the world he lives in. This may be a compensatory habit from his abbreviated formal education, and it may be an echo of his revered grandfather's own love of books. In any event, Buster has made of himself far and away the most educated cutting-horse trainer there is. In any serious sense, he is vastly more learned than many of his clients, however exalted their stations in life. And apart from the intrinsic merits of his knowledge, there is a place for it in Buster's work; because an unbroke horse is original unmodeled clay that can be brought to a level of great beauty or else remain in its original muddy form, dully consuming protein with the great mass of living creatures on the planet, but a cutting horse is a work of art. Buster Welch once described his great champion Little Peppy as "the clearest-minded horse that ever looked through a bridle."

I think Buster was looking through the same bridle.

4
SUGAR

Years ago, I took a twelve-year-old broodmare that I owned to a cutting-horse clinic in Livingston, Montana. She was out of shape, and I didn't know what to expect. But I knew she had once been a cutting horse. When my turn came, I rode her into the herd of cattle that milled at the end of the arena.

All I had to do was cut one cow from the herd. But each one I tried slipped past me.

Already the mare had begun to change beneath me. I felt her heightened alertness, a flow of new energy. The reins with which I guided her required a lighter and lighter touch. Finally, only one cow stood in front of us. The mare's attention was riveted, and I no longer needed the reins at all.

When the cow tried to get back to the herd, I knew I would ride cutting horses for the rest of my life. With liquid quickness, the mare countered every move that the cow made. Riding her on a slack rein gave me a sense of controlled free fall. Centered between the ears of my horse as if in the sights of a rifle, the cow faked and dodged. Much of the time I didn't know where I was or where the cow was, and I was certainly no help to the horse. But by the time I picked up the reins to stop, I was addicted to the thrilling shared movement of cutting, sometimes close to violence, which was well beyond what the human body could ever discover on its own.

In ranch work, the cutting horse is used to sort out unproductive cows from the herd, to separate bulls, to replace heifers, and to bring out sick or injured cattle for treatment. The herd instinct of cattle is tremendously strong, and to drive out an individual cow and hold her against this tidal force, a horse must act with knowledge, physical skill, and precision. Otherwise, the cow escapes and returns to a thoroughly upset herd.

The day of the cutting horse as a common ranch tool is waning, and the training and use of cutting horses has become largely a sporting proposition. To deny this would be like claiming your old bird dog was just another food-gathering device you maintained to keep your kitchen humming. Still, there is beauty and grace in the cutting horse, as well as a connection to a world older than we are. Amazingly, cutting horses can be found in all states except Alaska, and competitions sanctioned by the National Cutting Horse Association are held in forty-four states.

As a sport, cutting has a low entry level. Anyone who is reasonably comfortable riding can get on a cutting horse, hang on tight to the saddle horn, and feel the satisfaction and excitement of sitting astride a trained cow horse. But the journey to competence can be very long, and the frustration can be extreme. You must learn to ride in a way that does not drag at the motion of a horse. The body language between you and the horse must be bright and clear. A polished cutter sits in the middle of the saddle, holding the saddle horn but not pushing on it, never slinging his weight or dropping a shoulder into the turns. This quiet, eye-of-the-storm riding style is not easily achieved on the back of a sudden-moving, half-ton athlete. But to violate this style is to take the horse's mind off his work and increase his vulnerability to the movements of the cow.

Cutting begins and ends with horses—the minds, bodies, and souls of horses. You have to have a deep love of horses to endure the training. If you don't sense a kind of magic watching a horse take two steps or put his nose under water or switch flies, there's no real point. Cow-horse people sometimes can't tell their horses from themselves. You either learn to look at the world through the eyes of a horse or you quit cutting.

I bought a bay filly named Sugar O Lynn in Alabama, and she was broken to ride by a good hand there and sent to my ranch in McLeod, Montana, in the spring of 1988, at the age of two. I wanted to train her myself. My wife, Laurie, and I compete in Montana on our mature or "open" cutting horses, usually six years or older. Competing on young horses, which are comparatively inexperienced and volatile, is quite different, and we had never done it successfully. Laurie had her own filly, April, wisely entrusted to Sam Shepard, a talented trainer in Hartford, Alabama.

I began to ride Sugar out in the country and tried to get her to be quiet and serious. She was good-hearted but wound fairly tight, would jump back from water and strange shapes. You wanted to have a deep seat on her if you were taking her on a long ride by yourself.

I started her in cattle work, and she came right along, though she worried about cows and sometimes kicked at them when I rode her in the herd. By fall, I could guide her to sort a cow from the herd and then drop the reins for a few turns and let Sugar work on her own. It surprised me how she faced the unknown with confidence.

That winter I had work that took me out of the state and later out of the country. I sent Sugar to Tom Campbell, a good cowboy in Brady, Montana, and he gave her back to me in the spring of 1990 much improved. I rode her through the summer and fall and used up every cow in our valley trying to teach Sugar to run, stop, and turn correctly.

Next we sorted the ranch's calves off their mothers, and I schooled Sugar on them. At first their speed frightened her, and she worked wide-eyed, with her head practically in my lap. Eventually she settled down and tried to understand the rapid little animals, but they often beat her. When we sold the calves in October, Sugar and I worked the mothers. This was like going back to kindergarten for her, and she handled these cattle almost nonchalantly. Her big dark eyes sparkled with pleasure.

By this time, we could move quietly in the herd and sort out an individual cow. Sugar would run, stop, and turn intensely to hold the cow, but without continuing guidance from the reins she would soon get lost. Cows would head-fake her or press her back and run into the herd.

In cutting-horse competition, the reins cannot be used after a cow is cut. To hold the cow away from the herd, the horse must work on a slack rein. I wanted to enter Sugar in the most prestigious of all cutting-horse events: the NCHA Futurity, an annual competition in Fort Worth for three-year-old horses that have never been shown before. The futurity was just a couple of months away and it was starting to snow. Hard as it was for me to admit, Sugar was still not a contest horse, any more than I was a real horse trainer.

I called my friend Buster Welch. If anyone could put my program on track, Buster could. I realized that he might not want another horse to ride, and even if he did, he might not like mine. Buster had had open-heart surgery two years earlier. When I called, he was ranching fifty thousand acres in addition to getting cutting horses ready for himself, his wife, and about half a dozen friends who, like me, wanted to get something done at the futurity.

I was fortunate that he took Sugar on. I knew what kind of cutting horses Buster liked, because he had told me. He liked them "steeped in background, never crippled, and never had their hearts broke." I had ridden Sugar plenty in her short life, and I hoped he would find that she qualified. I sent her down to Texas.

I gave Sugar about a week to get a good look at those snappy West Texas cattle while Buster worked with her. Then I called Buster. His thoughts were composed. "Tom, I believe you held on to the reins too long," he said. "If you ride two-handed too long, a horse will stay a bronc all his life. When Sugar got here, I thought she couldn't outrun a fat man, but I guess she was only tired. I've shortened up her stride and quickened her moves wherever I could. You had a beautiful stop on her, but they really don't pay you to stop in Fort Worth."

He paused and let me take all this in. "She's got all the speed that is required," he continued, "and she is not going to quit us. You never gave her more than she wanted or could understand."

I wondered if I had given her enough to understand. Then Buster added, "But if they call from Fort Worth and want to put the futurity back a month, say yes."

I headed for Sweetwater by way of Abilene, Texas, to meet Buster and practice before heading for Fort Worth. The futurity has various divisions, but the principal ones are the non-professional class and the open, which is primarily for trainers. I was getting ready for the non-pro, and I had bitten off all I could chew.

I flew into Abilene at night and tried to rent a car that I could drop off in Fort Worth. Not everyone wanted me to do that. It was late and the small airport was quiet. I found one agency with a car that could be left in Fort Worth, but its plates were expired. "Expired back in October," said the pleasant woman, biting a wide mint patty. "Sittin' out there since then."

I went to another counter. I didn't see anyone. I looked around, and then something behind the counter caught my attention. The agent, a woman around thirty, was asleep on the floor. I noticed her shoes neatly arranged on the counter, which was, I suppose, a way of telling customers she had turned in. She sensed my presence and stood up, rubbing the sleep from her eyes. "I got to catch a nap whenever I can," she said. "Some folks prod me awake with their foot. Ain't that cold?"

After being assured that I could leave the car in Fort Worth, I asked her to direct me to Sweetwater, and she told me the way to Highway 20. "Go forty-five miles and be sure not to blink," she said.

"Are you going back to sleep?" I asked.

"I'm up now," she said.

The next morning I wandered around Sweetwater, admired its pleasant neighborhoods and numerous churches. The streets had cast-iron manhole covers that said DO NOT MOLEST, a useful general remark. I stopped in a cafe for breakfast, and when my waffles came, they were embossed with a map of Texas.

These waffles take us to Texas pride, which is not fixing to die. The so-called chauvinism of Texas, which I find to be a hearty pride of heritage, is a booming and immodest thing. It brings grand rejuvenating powers to its citizens. Texas is an oasis of undamaged egos, a place where Birkenstocks, oat bran, foreign films, and Saabs spontaneously catch fire and then smolder grimly in an alien climate.

I gave Buster a call. I wanted to find out when he was coming to town with the horses to practice in the Nolan County Coliseum. "You better come out here and help me," he said over his truck radio. "If you-all want me to come to Sweetwater tomorrow and help you, you've got to help me today."

I missed a turn heading out to Buster's place and pulled into a ranch yard to ask for directions. It turned out to be a large breeding kennel for Chihuahuas, and when I got out of my car, they swarmed toward me at ankle height, driving me back inside. I decided I had better find my own way.

Buster's ranch is in the middle of some of the prettiest land I'd ever seen in Texas, winding caliche roads, deeply cut red-banked riverbeds, country that looked pink and green in a certain light. I complimented Buster on his property. "It's outdoors," he said, "all of it."

We loaded three-year-old bulls and carried them around the ranch in a stock trailer, vaccinating them and dropping them off wherever Buster wanted. Betweentimes, Buster issued commands over the truck radio and speculated about our horses, for whom we all had such high hopes. Of his own stallion, Peppy Olé, Buster said, "God has decided to give Buster Welch one more good horse."

Meanwhile, Laurie and April had gone to Ardmore, Oklahoma, to practice for the futurity. I had no idea if Laurie was gaining an advantage or falling behind me, because things occur in Oklahoma that are clothed in secrecy. We had wished each other luck, knowing that many of the sorest issues of the age lay in the outcome of our competition. If, for example, Laurie won the futurity and I fell off my horse, nothing anyone could say would help me. If I won and Laurie fell off her horse, some of the things that have caused the pots and pans to fly around our house in the last few years would be with us again.

The next morning, early, Buster and I were in the coliseum along with fifty young cutting horses, their riders, and plenty of crossbred cattle. I rode Sugar around for a while; it was good to be on her familiar back again. Then I joined Buster as he watched his son Greg work a horse he had trained, a quick, attentive stud, perfectly prepared.

In a cutting-horse competition, judges evaluate the performances of horses and riders as if they were working on an open range. A herd of about sixty cattle is brought into an arena and settled along the back fence. Two mounted herd holders are stationed on either side of the herd, and a pair of mounted turn-back riders are in front, prepared to keep the cattle that have been cut focused on returning to the herd. The mounted cutter enters the herd and selects a cow to drive out. He then must control the cow until he releases her and cuts another. He has two and a half minutes to cut either two or three cattle. The rider is awarded points based on how cleanly he makes each cut, how well he controls the cow afterward, and how difficult the cow is to handle.

A cutting horse not only has to be quicker than the cow but also has to have the strategic sense to deal with the cow's bold first moves. The rider, through weight shifts and other body signals (such as leg pressure and touches of the spurs), can tell the horse what he thinks the cow will do. The rider must also react without interference to moves the horse devises on his own. These shared signals constitute the elusive "feel" of cutting.

As Greg schooled his horse, Buster explained things to me. "Pick up that cow, go with it," he said. "Shadow that cow. Don't get in a race. If you get in a race, let the cow win. And when you're cutting a cow, stalk it. That will tell your horse what you are up to."

Then a trainer named Gary Bellenfant worked a mare on three different hard-running cows without ever having to raise the rein to make an adjustment. Buster remarked that we might just as well be trying to make violins. It took thousands of hours, no matter how smart and talented you were, to train a cutting horse. The horse had to see so many cattle, and he had to grow up and experience the world enough for new places not to terrify him and prevent him from doing his work. These cutting horses were, after all, excitable young animals who were being asked to do and understand a lot.

Buster's wife, Sheila, worked her horse cleanly, quietly. "Next time I get on her will be at Fort Worth," she said afterward. She was back on her the next day. In the uninterfering style of riding that Buster advocates, Sheila excels from long practice and tutelage and her own competitive spirit.

During my week in Sweetwater I took long hikes in the mesquite-dotted hills, watched fifty horses work a day, rode Sugar, and felt how far she'd come under Buster's saddle, and by the end of the week I was close to chewing wood. I was amazed at the ability of some seasoned cutters to go into a state of suspended animation for days on end in the coliseum's bleachers. On Thanksgiving there was a general retreat to the cavelike twilight of motel rooms for football games. I decided a change of cuisine was in order and deserted Whataburger for McDonald's, where I spent part of Thanksgiving evening listening to a spirited debate between two old farmers about Jack Ruby.

It was time to head for Fort Worth. I drove east through country given over mainly to cotton, with large cotton wagons that gleaned the bolls from windrows in the fields. There was a beautiful big sun out, and soft, indefinite clouds. The hours on the highway isolated my hopes for the futurity and then twisted them into baseless fears: I can't get my horse into the coliseum because I can't find the gate; I ride Sugar around Fort Worth in a traffic jam, unable to reach an off-ramp; my chaps blow over my face while I'm trying to cut cattle, and I can't find the herd in the deafening laughter. Various bursts of demoralizing nonsense.

Laurie arrived in Fort Worth from Oklahoma, and we went to a pleasant Italian restaurant on Camp

Bowie Boulevard called Sardine's, where she described every good horse she had seen in Ardmore, and I described every good horse I had seen in Sweetwater.

"How's your horse?" I asked.

"Solid. How's yours?"

"Hotter than a two-dollar pistol. Did you have any problems?"

"Did you?"

"Let's just enjoy our meal," I said. She seemed to be regarding me, twirling her pasta fork in the air and sizing me up. Cutting is a sport for the whole family.

Laurie was assigned to ride on November 26, the first day of the futurity. The day before, Will Rogers coliseum was surrounded by horse trucks and trailers with license plates from across the nation. I walked in and looked around the coliseum's spacious interior, a venerable place to cutters. The bleachers were empty, the judges' boxes untenanted. I sat down close to the rail and remembered a night thirteen years earlier, when Buster had won the futurity on Little Peppy: I had never seen anything like it in my life, the mercurial speed of that young stallion, his impact on a coliseum filled with people who had nothing on their minds but a love of cutting horses. It would seem like a privilege to ride my young mare onto that sand—win, lose, or draw.

Laurie had a nice controlled run that assured her of a slot in the second go-round. I couldn't help but notice how quietly she cut her cows and how lightly she sat on her quick little horse. I wouldn't work until the next day, so I watched and tried to make myself memorize individual cattle in the herd.

Heather Stiles had a fine run on a horse Buster had trained. Heather, a high school senior, has grown up on the one-and-a-quarter-million-acre King Ranch in South Texas, where her father is in charge of the cattle. She is a natural rider and a remarkably serious individual. I would have been quite pleased if Heather had won the non-pro class and its $35,454 first prize. I even had generous thoughts about Laurie getting to the finals or even winning. So many horses were making their way through the go-rounds, 165 in the non-pro alone, that no one really cared what happened to you until you did enough to suggest that it would be a shame if you failed.

Nevertheless, there was a feeling of intense scrutiny; and indeed the five judges, sequestered in their towers, clipboards on their knees, were looking at the riders very closely.

Sometimes it helped just to walk around and visit with people. I watched a few runs with Ned Huntt, a cutter from Maryland who has ridden all his life. He is in the landscaping business. He lost an arm in his late teens and, unable to hold the saddle horn, he rides as we all should, by sheer balance. He was watching the clock, waiting for his turn. Ned and I talked about the difficulty of controlling all the variables in cutting competition, like your place in the draw, the mood of your horse, the freshness of your cattle, and the quality of the herd holders and turn-back riders. Ned thought these variables were the most daunting aspect of the sport, the thing that took the pleasure out of it for some cutters.

I watched a few runs with Spencer Harden, who trains his own horses in Millsap, Texas, though he's a non-professional. Last year he won the open class, an extremely rare occurrence for a non-pro.

I walked around and ran into L. H. Wood standing in line to buy a cup of coffee. He trains border collies, and I have one of his dogs, Ella H., a useful ranch dog and gifted beggar of table scraps. He shows horses trained by his son Kobie and has been a frequent futurity finalist. He didn't look as nervous as I felt. He backed up to a wall and made his hat rise on his head as if by magic while he inflated his cheeks.

The alarm went off the morning of my first go-round. The shower in the residential hotel had no hot water, and I woke up too fast. As I tried to get a quick snack for breakfast, the toaster caught fire. I headed for the coliseum. Matt Lopez, a Sioux cowboy who works for Buster, was riding Sugar around. I took Sugar from Matt and joined the competitors loping in a circle to warm up. Matt said, "Good luck."

Suddenly my name was called, and I was riding toward the herd. Behind me, I heard a woman's voice say, "Load the wagon and don't mind the mules!" Was she talking to me?

As we passed the judges, Sugar craned around and had a good look at them. She was filled with suspicion. Apparently, my horse was confident. Once we were in the herd, I felt better. We rode around and moved some cattle out in front of us. One particular black cow looked fresh, head up and not out of breath. She stood and let us cut her. The rest of the herd moved quietly away and behind us.

I put my reining hand down. The cow realized she was alone. She made a hard run to the right, spun, and went the other way. I felt that first magical hard break that a cutting horse makes with a cow, the hindquarters sinking into the stop so that the floor of the arena seems to rise sharply around you, and suddenly you're going the other way. It is an exhilarating movement, akin to flight.

Sugar handled this cow correctly, with good hard stops, staying right with her, nose to nose. Then we cut a wild motley-faced cow that nearly sent us home. I could feel Sugar get a bit lost as the pace picked up. The cow didn't respect anything Sugar did, and Sugar's confidence was eroding. She became unsure of the correct way to do things and desperate as she tried to beat the cow to the stops. She became much harder to ride.

We made the second go-round by the skin of our teeth. I was going to have to make up a lot of ground if I hoped to reach the semifinals. And I knew Sugar was rattled.

Larry Mahan, in a tweed coat and cardigan sweater, arrived to watch the competition. A six-time world-champion rodeo cowboy, he's now a good non-professional cutting-horse rider. Mahan took on this sport with becoming modesty, given his credentials in rodeo. When riding broncs or bulls, he says, "You sublimate everything in order to react to what happens; you just kind of gas it for eight seconds. You get to where you even divorce yourself from that guy out there making the ride. But with cutting horses, you have to find a harmony with the horse. You have to reflect that horse's energy, and he has to reflect yours. You have to be sharp. You have to react. But the thing you have to have is the feel."

And the feel could come from anywhere—your attitude, the demeanor of the animal, the smell of the sweat on the horse's shoulders, the look in his eye, the electric suddenness of his moves. You could never be sure who had that feel. It might well be somebody's grandmother.

A young Californian, Phil Rapp, riding a horse he had trained, won the first go-round with a run that suggested he and his horse could go the entire distance. A curious thing happens in cutting: if your start is wobbly, you begin to shift your attention to horses and riders who seem more deserving of success. The hope of virtue being rewarded is part of the atmosphere.

In the second go-round, on November 29, Laurie had another nice run. Her horse was so intense, so locked down in her stops, that people cheered. Laurie was headed for the semis. With a better-than-average run, I could join her there, and we could compete in an atmosphere of good sportsmanship, our entry fees won back and our earlier scores erased, a clean slate. As I rode Sugar around, warming up amid a stream of galloping horses, I listened to the announcer and began to feel comfortable. A little positive thinking was coming into my consciousness.

And then I was walking toward the herd. It was now or never. Heather Stiles had been eliminated when she was nearly run over by a black cow with a red ear tag, and I was trying to follow the cow's progress in the herd to be sure I didn't cut her. As I watched the cattle melt away in front of me until one was isolated, I dropped my hand. I waited for that decisive move that mirrors the first break of the cow, but it never came. Sugar jumped sharply to my right, toward the wrong cow.

It was over.

I walked across the warm-up pen. Another cutter was already working. At least at an event this big you get to have your defeat to yourself. When I climbed into the bleachers, I looked back at Sugar tied to the rail, one back foot tipped up, asleep. She had her whole life ahead of her. I knew, absolutely, that she was a good horse.

Suddenly, though, I was a pedestrian, a cheerleader. By the time the semifinals rolled around the next night, I was accustomed to my new role, even looking forward to it. But Laurie overrode her horse trying to hold a tough cow and went off the end—the horse never stopped, and the cow cut back to the herd behind her. Laurie was eliminated, and soon we would be homeward bound.

I sat for a while in the bleachers. Time was certainly not flying. I ran into Ian Tyson, a singer-songwriter friend from Alberta. The previous year he had reached the futurity finals, before, as he put it, being hammered by gum-chewing California girls with ice water in their veins. It was nice to hear a lighter view of something you have spent so long trying to do and failed at. "Well, Ian, what are you working on?" I asked.

Ian thought for a moment and, seeming to focus on something in a faraway but pleasant place, smiled and said, "I'm working on a reggae about magpies."

I felt better already.

Laurie and I stayed to watch the finals the next night. Sheila Welch and a number of other people we knew were among the twenty remaining riders. Phil Rapp did not make the finals on his great young mare. Heather Stiles looked depressed. We saw a couple of real heartbreakers as good horses and riders got beaten by treacherous cows.

Spencer Harden again did brilliantly, finishing second in the non-pro division. Matt Gaines, a college student from Stephenville, Texas, and a lifelong cutter, won. When I spoke to him later, I got the feeling he would never quite believe he had won. Matt talked about his heroes, including his father, who had helped him train his horse. I could see Matt had little chance of escaping his dream of understanding these horses and the open-range skills they celebrated.

I remembered the previous year's weekend cuttings, through a summer's endless golden progress, the ten o'clock sundowns when I walked Sugar through the cottonwood shadows to cool her down. Listening to this young champion, it all came back, that search for something in a horse and in myself.

5

ANOTHER HORSE

Gene was sure there were enough horses. When I called him I said my friend Scott wanted to come and we would need another horse. I told him I had the saddles: a Mexican roping saddle and a slick-fork, marked Montana Territory, in case we met any antiquarians in the mountains.

I drove south in the Yellowstone Valley the next morning; Scott got the gate and we headed up the road to the ranch that Gene stays on. It was a cold late-November day; Gene and Keith were putting the horses in the stock truck to take them up to the trail-head in Tom Miner Basin. Gene had a bandanna tied around the crown of his hat to ward off nimrods and was wearing green chaps he won bull-riding in Willis-ton, North Dakota, in 1965 (it said so on the chaps). He was wearing a gun.

Keith was dressed in his National Park Service coveralls and it was he who discovered we were shy a horse. Scott and I were hikers, though not so committed that we'd forgo the one horse to share. I said we'd take that and they could pack our gear in the panniers and we'd meet them in camp.

Keith had secreted his little camp up some six-inch creek in the Gallatin Range; so we all hunkered around a clean patch of bare mud and scratched out directions. I made sure Scott and I had matches. We were going through an area of some grizzly concentration. I don't know what you bring for that.

We put the territorial saddle on a bunchy short mare that jumped every time you took off your coat, Gene said, though she was "a good little bitch"; and I noticed she tipped up her left hind hoof when you walked around her. He said she pulled back all the time when you used her in the pack string; and once when Gene had tried to cure her by securing her to his pickup truck with a logging chain instead of a rope, she reared until she broke the logging chain. Then didn't go anywhere.

"What kind of logging chain, Gene?"

"Just a damn logging chain."

I wanted to wear my John B. Stetson hat with the big feather in it; but my ears hurt already, so I put the hat away and with it a certain portion of my self-esteem and pulled on a woolen hat instead.

Keith and Jim (another fellow from Bozeman) headed off in the pickup carrying the pack saddles, panniers, and all the gear. Scott and I went with Gene in the stock truck. When we got halfway down the ranch road, Gene spotted his dogs following us in the rearview mirror. He hit the brakes, jumped out of the truck, drew his gun, and fired. The dogs hightailed it for the house. I looked at Scott. The woolen hat was itching me already.

We crossed the Yellowstone and headed up Tom Miner Basin, struggling for traction on the long, snowy canyon road. We parked the trucks at the top. Somebody had a tent there; and there was a small corral with four bales of hay in the snow.

Jim said, "Can you throw a diamond hitch?" I said I could.

Scott and I led the four saddle horses and the two packhorses up to the corral and tied them. There was a lot of snow and we would be going up another three or four thousand feet, Scott and I trading off on the antiquarian saddle, both being too big to double-team the twitchy mare.

Some hunters came up to the head of the road in a little jeep, packed inside, all guns and hot-orange hats.

"I don't see nothin' hangin'," said the driver.

"We're only starting out," one of us said; though the truth was, Scott and I were just going to make a bloodless round-trip to see the Gallatins under snow.

Gene knew where Keith's camp was for sure. Scott and I knew where it was on the mud map back at Gene's place; but there was more snow than we thought there would be and trails would be obscured. So Gene went ahead to cut a trail. Jim and Keith agreed to pack up and follow when they were done; and meanwhile Scott and I would start, trading off on the mare.

We started up the easy grade along Tom Miner Creek, Scott getting the first ride, up through the bare aspens and gradual snow-covered slopes dotted by dark knots of sage. We could see the snowy Absaroka Range across the Yellowstone.

Then the canyon steepened during my turn on the horse, as I saw Scott fade, trudging behind in six inches of snow. The trail contoured around high on the north side, really quite steep; and I remembered two years before in the summertime with Keith, taking two riding horses and a three-year-old that had never been packed between us, me in front. The young horse banged the plywood panniers on a tree and panicked, chasing my horse head-long down the skinny trail, the creek sonorous in the deep canyon below me. Finally, my horse swerved up on a short leveling of the slope and stood crooked and not half so unnerved as I. The young packhorse shot on through, bucking and emptying the panniers of everything from sleeping bags to Pepsodent and a German chocolate cake. The cake made a long, tumbling bounce and then vaporized against a spruce tree.

Today it was relaxed, with the snow muffling the horse's hoofs and the altitude beginning, in the cold air, to produce the radiant and astringent combination of air and light that is year after year fecklessly pursued by the manufacturers of beer calendars. I noticed that riding was colder than walking; my toes were a little numb, as were my nose and cheek points; my ears, thankfully, were warm, due entirely to the abandoning of my High Lonesome hat down there at headquarters. I stopped and waited for Scott. The horse looked out on the snowscape and I remember feeling a peculiar responsibility toward her as though she were a child to whom the reason for this trip had never been explained.

When Scott caught up, he confessed to thinking about grizzlies. "If one came after me," he said, "I would dodge around in those aspens, in and out, in and out, until somebody came and rescued me."

I trudged along behind as he gradually disappeared ahead. The snow was getting heavy; and now the sky was deeply overcast and snow was beginning to pour down the canyon in a long sweep. After a while, I could see it streaming into the horse tracks, obscuring them. I transferred the matches to an inside pocket and mentally reviewed Jack London. I thought, When I get back, I'm going to buy a whole mess of horses so we never run out.

My eyes flicked to the brushy creek bottom for grizzly sign; just like one of those fang mongers to come on a man having a hard enough time as it was. I had the strange thought that nothing could happen to a person by way of grizzer charge or vanishment beneath snowbank who had as many magazine subscriptions as I do. But it was getting to be grim out here. I could see about fifteen inches ahead of me.

The snow was deep enough that it was a struggle to walk, and my boots were full. If I had stayed home, I could have watched the Colts and Dolphins play, up in my room with snacks and the Sunday *Livingston Enterprise* and cozy telephone calls to my friend the writer down the road as to the relative greatnesses of Tolstoy and Dostoevsky. Or I could read an off-color comic from San Francisco. I could tie a fly for next summer.

I caught up with Scott in about half an hour. I climbed on the horse, not describing to him what he was in for. I noticed, though, that my boots disappeared into the snow, stirrups and all, making wakes. Scott remarked the horse looked like a cocktail waitress. So it was beginning to get to him, too.

In two trade-offs, we made it to the top. We looked back into the immense valley of the Yellowstone and rode (or walked) through the trees on a kind of plateau, Buffalo Horn Pass, where the Indian hunting parties crossed; and then to the western slope and a tremendous view of the Gallatin drainage with white, jagged ranges angling in from the north.

The snow let up and we were in deep powder. When it was my turn to ride, I started down a long switchback that ended in the trees. Scott, on foot, decided to run straight down. At about the point I reached the trees, Scott was pinwheeling in a cloud of snow. Then the horse fell. Fearing getting hung up in the stirrups, I ejected before she hit the ground. The snow was so deep and soft that Scott and I and the horse wallowed around and made no very great attempt to get to our feet again.

The sun came out and the raucous birds of the high mountains started in with some brazen appreciation of the general improvement.

The horse was getting silly. When one of us rode ahead and the other reappeared, she jumped back in horror as though from a representative of a dog-food concern. And on the steep switchbacks, she slid down the snow on her haunches. I felt she was stunting and might pull anything next, an Immelmann turn, for example.

Then Scott galloped off through the trees, the trail making a soft white corridor and the speed of his departure producing a sun-shot curtain of snow. The laden boughs poured white powder in the sunshine; whole sections of snow dropped from the treetops onto the trail with a soft concussion. Suddenly we were in camp: a wall tent half buried in powder and a pole corral.

Gene was cutting "standing dead" for the sheepherder stove in the tent and we took turns splitting it. Keith and Jim arrived almost immediately with the pack stock. Keith complained that Gene had cut the trail too close to the trees, so that the pack animals banged the panniers all the way up; then, to Scott and me, he allowed as how the snow had been unexpectedly deep. He was speaking to us but you could still sense his annoyance at Gene.

"Did the horse fall?"

"Yes."

"I saw the place. See any game?"

"Gene saw two moose."

Jim said, "The sorrel packhorse fell and slid forty feet on its stomach and got up straight without spilling anything."

We all admired that.

"How many of these horses you want to picket?" Gene asked Keith. Keith looked around. It didn't look like we could get by losing even one if the weather kept falling apart.

"All of them," Keith said. "Then let's butcher up a good mess of wood. It's going to get cold."

The sun was starting to go down. We had one more tent to put up. It took an hour to shovel the snow out of the site and get the ridgepole in place. The pile of split wood, fresh and lemony smelling, was building in front of the first tent. And by about sundown the second tent was up, the heater in place. We threw in two shovelfuls of dirt so the bottom wouldn't burn out; put the sheet-metal tubes together to form the chimney and ran it up through the asbestos hole in the roof. We built a fire in it; and the snow inside started to melt in the warmth and form the mud hell that was necessary until the tent had aged a few days.

We went to the other tent about sundown. It was very cold; we started to work on making dinner, spacing the job out with bourbon and one of those ersatz wines that is advertised right in there at halftime with Gillette razors and the Dodge Rebellion. Some of us were swaggering around with cigars. We were never able to smell the food cooking.

Scott and I peeled potatoes and onions. Keith and Gene cooked some elk, sliced up a head of lettuce with a hunting knife. Jim explained how he had expelled Allen Ginsberg from a coffeehouse for running down America. "No way I put up with that," said Jim.

We ate, greedily, for the first time that day. The mud was starting to deepen in the tent.

Somebody hauled some feed to the horses; I looked out the tent flaps and saw them picking precisely through the snow with their front hoofs for the pellets.

I was pouring bourbon into cups full of powder snow; Keith would drink half a can of 7UP and pour whiskey down through the triangular hole into the can and say, "Right on!" to no one in particular.

Gene rose imperfectly to his feet and began doing six-gun tricks, whirls, drops, spin-and-draws, fanning back the hammer.

"Is that loaded?" I peeped.

"Yes."

We all backed away into the corners, fearing a general O.K. Corral. Finally, Gene, winded, put the gun back in its holster.

Jim dropped his elk steak on the floor. When he picked it up, it was covered with mud and had a few mothballs stuck to it. "Go ahead and eat it," everyone encouraged him. He said he wasn't hungry. He shook it over the fire until the mothballs fell off and took a couple of bites anyway.

Jim took the bucket of heated water off the sheepherder stove and started washing the dishes. In passing, he explained that Dave Brubeck liked to pinch girls' bottoms, figured he could get by with it.

"Where's Keith?" I asked.

No one knew. After a while, I went to look for him. He was asleep in the other tent, laid out in the mud in his sleeping bag next to a pile of saddles. I put a couple of pieces of wood into the heater and the base of the chimney glowed cherry. When I walked back to the other tent, I stopped in the cold, still air and looked up at the stars. They seemed to swarm a matter of inches over my head. I guessed they'd been there all along but when you're in your house you don't notice.

Scott came out. "That's Orion," he said. "See the belt and the sword there?"

I said I did; but the truth is, I never could make those things out much, beyond the Big and Little Dippers and the North Star if I didn't take my eyes off of it. I heard a coyote. I thought, I am on top of the earth and I don't work for the government. Then waited til the coyote let loose again, a little different, always a little different as the song evolved.

Jim, Gene, and Keith all slept in the same tent because they were going to get up before dawn to look for elk. Scott and I rolled out our bags on the floor and turned off the Coleman lantern. For about half an hour, we could hear the banked-down stove crackle and see the rectangle of bright light around its door.

When the stove went out, the mud froze. I wished I had flattened out some of the mud under my bag because it froze in shapes not reciprocal to my body. I pulled the drawstring up tight around my face. I was warm in the good Ibex bag; but my head felt as if it were in a refrigerator. I put on my wool cap, feeling for it among my frozen, board-stiff socks and the hiking boots that were as rigid as building blocks with their tongues stuck out stiff.

I could hear when I woke up the next morning the other three crunching around outside, wrangling the horses and falling silent as they drank coffee in the tent. It was insultingly cold.

Scott said, "Oh, no!" from the interior of his sleeping bag.

"What?"

"I have to go to the bathroom."

We got up shortly and had a crackling fire going in the sheepherder stove. We made a pot of coffee and lazily divided a vast sheet of Missus So-and-So's breakfast rolls. I thawed my socks and boots in front of the stove; rivers of steam poured from them into the stove's open door.

When I stepped outside, I could see where the snow was trampled from the morning's wrangling. Their trail led across the small open meadow and over the rim, a soft trough in the perfect basin of snow. The light was tremendous, and the sky formed an impressive light-shot blue dome, defined on the side of our camp by a row of snow-laden pines, and opposite us by the glittering range of the Gallatins. A big lone spruce stood between us and the newly risen sun; full of snow and ice crystals, it exploded with the improbable brilliance of the Annunciation. There weren't words for it.

We put the sleeping bags in stuff sacks, straightened out the tent, and let the fire die. I printed a note and left it on a pannier, weighted with a jackknife.

Boys,
We're going to work our way back. We'll
leave the horse in the corral at Tom Miner
Basin.

Tom and Scott

We got the bridle and saddle and headed out for the mare. A pine bough had shed its load of snow and her back was white and powdered with it as she stood in the glittering mountain light. I swept her dry while Scott warmed the bit in his hands.

We saddled the mare and took the long way home. She didn't seem to be in much of a rush.

6

THE LIFE AND HARD TIMES OF CHINK'S BENJIBABY

Since the days of the trail drives, a horse with the mind and physical ability to sort sick cattle and strays from large herds has had great practical value and is usually ridden by the most accomplished cowman in the outfit. Individual cattle don't want to leave the herd, however admirable the reasons, and they are quick and clever enough to test the horses trying to drive them out. As for the rider, there really isn't time to rein the horse from one spot to another, moving the cattle. Once the cut has been made, it's up to the horse to make the reflexive decisions necessary to drive the cow into the open.

It has long been correct for even the most "horse-back" rider to hold on to the horn; the stresses, G-forces, and lateral loads on the rider make it necessary. Gradually, under the pressure of wagering, a controlled contest evolved so that one cutting horse

could be tested against another, one rider against another; and the unanswerable question arose as to who
was to get the credit, horse or rider. It is said that a
great cutting-horse rider can always trade horses with
you and beat you. It is also assumed that the horse
does it all. The truth is that the relationship between
horse and rider is so intricate that one of the funda-
mental problems of a cutting-horse rider lies in
controlling his own mood. Controlling your mood
when a horse turns so sharply as to stick your spur in
the ground is occasionally a matter of controlling fear.

Over the years, there have been legendary cutting
horses: Jesse James, Poco Lena, Sugar Vaquero, Little
Peppy, and Hollywood Gold, among the modern
greats. And in my time, a mysterious black mare, re-
ported to be crazy, Chink's Benjibaby, the product of
rejection and indomitable greatness, a horse who has
waged unremitting mind war against cutting-horse
riders, especially trainers.

Why would anyone call a horse Chink's Benjibaby? Well, her mother's name was Chink and her
father was the old cutting-horse stallion named King
Benjiman, who in his old age was my ranch stallion.
She was born in California in vaguely suburban circumstances of the densest kind of Texas blood, King
and the legendary Old Sorrel. And her subsequent
history would indicate that she was not born for life
in the Golden West. Her original owners had her in a

chain-link pen and threw her feed over the top. She was considered unpredictable even as a baby. But her refined face and slick-black form highlighted in chestnut maintained a tenuous line of credit for a horse destined to drive people to desperate frustration.

One early owner complained that she destroyed his box stall. So he had a contractor build one of cinder block. She tore that down, and the contractor, who had guaranteed the stall would hold her, accused the new owner of being a psychopath who stole out at night with a pickax to tear down his work. When the new owner decided to haul her to a cutting, Chink's Benjibaby disliked her trailer and destroyed it. And yet, from the beginning, no one suspected her of meanness. It was agreed that she was a kind and capable horse who hated confinement and machinery. There was a feeling that because of the general deficiencies of the twentieth century, she was not fully responsible for her actions.

Nevertheless, for the first time in her life, Chink's began to be rejected. Her conduct was sometimes amusing, as when she stood up on her hind legs like a kangaroo and watched the humans, or, when boredom overtook her in her box stall, she decided to leave hoofprints on the walls, twelve feet off the ground. But sometimes a darker mania overtook her, and she raised Cain until her eyeballs rolled and she fell soaked with sweat into a deep and troubled sleep.

Some said that she wasn't meant for a life in stalls and pens, that she was a cowboy's horse and that in any case, nobody would know what she was until they stopped crossing her. She had more than met people halfway by letting them ride her.

Jerry Vawter, a prominent West Coast stallion man, first saw Chink's Benjibaby at Rancho California as a green cutting horse who had nothing to show for herself but her desire and chaotic genius. To a less practiced eye, she was probably ridiculous. Impatient with slow cattle, she reared, sank on her hocks, and vibrated in the hopes of getting something done for herself and for her rider, breaking all the rules, but revealing the intensity of "cow"— that quality of inclination to break down and work cattle—that Vawter remembered from her great sire, King Benjiman, whom the part-Indian Ray Thomas had ridden to glory on the West Coast. Vawter bought the horse immediately. He sold her soon thereafter.

Bill Baldwin, a cutting-horse photographer as well as a rider, took Chink's on trial. He concluded that she was great if you had time to ride her twenty miles to take the edge off before you went cutting. She walked the fence all night like a stallion and seemed to have some intense drive that no one could focus. "She was a cowboy's horse," said Bill, "and I didn't feel cowboy enough to keep her."

Chink's Benjibaby was shipped to two different cutting-horse trainers in the Southwest, top hands each, and was promptly rejected. Finally, a man in Kansas bought her and hauled her to Pat Jacobs of Gate, Oklahoma, for a last try; but the Kansas man went bankrupt and the most ignominious thing that can happen to a horse happened to this unlucky mare: she was repossessed by the bank. Banks like to liquidate collateral and a horse without obvious utility can well end up at the canners.

What happened to Chink's Benjibaby after that is the subject of contradictory stories. I had been interested in the mare since acquiring her half sister, Benjistripe, another brilliant horse. Later we bought King Benjiman, her sire, and hauled him here to Montana, and thus became the recipients of Chink's Benjibaby lore. When Pat Jacobs invited us to Gate for Thanksgiving, my wife and I decided to go for a number of reasons: one of them was to find out what happened to Chink's after the bank got her. The other, as Pat promised, was to eat wild turkey and drink Wild Turkey.

Gate is in the Oklahoma panhandle. And the only way we could get there that weekend was by small plane. Things are a little slower in that part of the world. The front bedroom of Pat's last lease-ranch, for instance, was the former office of the Dodge City–to–Tascosa, Texas, stage line. When you come in from the west across the flat farmland of eastern

Colorado and western Kansas, the monotony of rec-
tangles and center-pivot sprinklers is hypnotically
boring. Then it changes and the whorls of seasonal
runoff in the empty sand hills, all russet against a pale
fall horizon, have a beauty unmarred by the weathered
homes and corrals of ranchers who are there to stay.

We dipped over Pat's ranch to let him know we'd be
landing soon. I could see the rows of stalls and runways.
Every runway had a cutting horse, and the sight seemed
incredibly exotic: these ponies are as strange and special
as falcons. In one pen, a curious black figure ran in circles at the sound of the airplane: Chink's Benjibaby.

The aerial view of the Oklahoma panhandle and
the wonderful topography gave way as we made our
approach, and soon the bare horizon was all that
stood out around the little airfield. In a moment, Pat
was there, muddy M. L. Leddy boots to his knees,
spurs jingling.

Pat is a cattle trader and cutting-horse trainer. Most
trainers now are assembled around big population
centers—Dallas–Fort Worth, Phoenix, Los Angeles—
where displaced people spend money on cutting
horses out of some kind of regional memory. Pat still
lives out in the sticks, trading feeder cattle. He still believes that the King- and Leo-bred horses, who are the
foundation of the sport, are better than the omni-
present Doc Bars, who represent the impact of California on the world of cutting. I see him leading a Doc

Bar stud; the horse refuses to go into the arena: "This sumbuck's got so much cow he can't go in there and face it." Pat won't ride the fashionable Buster Welch saddles because of their flat seats, and rides instead a Price McLauchlin stock saddle with a built-up ground seat, claiming the Buster Welch model was designed to accommodate the inventor's hemorrhoids. And he likes to see a horse athlete enough, like the great Sugar Vaquero, to blow by a cow a little before cracking around, to master the cow even in the difficult corners, as opposed to trying to win in the middle, however elegantly, with what the old Spanish bullfighters referred to contemptuously as "dancing."

This is not the modern school, where the trainer meets you at the airport in a limousine. Pat's forte is open horses, the mature cutting horses who go down the road year after year, who stay tough until eighteen and older. Some might think it unfashionable, when cutting today is focused on the futurities, where three-year-old horses are shown for the first and sometimes the last time. At three, Chink's Benjibaby was still walking on her back legs. She was destined to be an open horse or die in a can.

Pat lives with his wife, Nellie, his contraction of Ganell, her real name. When they were dating in the fifties, he was simultaneously seeing a girl named Raynell and he feared getting his sweet nothings crossed up. I never met Raynell, but I am sure Ganell was the right idea. She had been riding with him, turning back cattle, and helping with his colts for eighteen years when I went to visit. By now, it's thirty-eight.

The house is obviously the residence of cutting-horse mania. There is a big wall clock made out of trophy buckles, and trophy saddles are scattered around. The panhandle horizon is visible out any window. There is a desk set cornerwise, with a phone, notepads, and pocket calculator, everything a cattle trader needs: the rest is under his hat or better be.

This is cattle country. The country seems shaped to that fact; that, and oil. The pragmatists learn the business by the seat of their pants, or at the hands of an older trader. That's what Pat did, swapping cattle out of an abandoned Champion gas station. The romantics head south to ride the rough string on ranches like the Four Sixes or Swenson's or the Matador. Everybody cries when they hear Bob Wills do "Faded Love." As to oil, here and there is some old kid living off a hundred thousand a month out of those iron jackrabbits pumping crude in the pastures his father and uncles pushed cattle all over, never suspecting it was there. There are good old kids and bad old kids who fly stewardesses up from Oklahoma City three at a time and have rooms with purple walls, round sofas, and decorative planting to protect them from that empty panhandle horizon.

The subject of Bob Wills, the master of Texas swing, comes up as we are sitting in a little bottle club on the Texas-Oklahoma line. We are guests of Frankie McWhorter, who broke horses for the Four Sixes and who is a master of Texas swing fiddle. On the way to the club, we dropped a horse with Frankie for him to "untrack" by riding her to cattle in the hills. A good young mare, she's been working in cattle pens so long she's forgotten how to lope. Pat used to travel with Lefty Frizzell's band as a guitarist, and this was an opportunity for Pat to give us his good rendition of "Please Release Me." Then he sits down. "When I was rodeoing," he says, "that was the lowest scum on earth. So I went into music and the ranchers thought that was sissy. I had an inferiority complex most of my life." Nellie looks at the ceiling and laughs.

Pat bought Chink's Benjibaby back from the bank. I asked, "How did you train the mare?" This was my big question.

"I didn't," says Pat. "I never won a fight."

Pat talked all through that weekend about this strange horse, about getting under her skin to form enough of a team to get somewhere. Part of the excitement of riding cutting horses is this quality of collaboration. Human beings are species-lonely, relying on needy pushovers like dogs and cats to connect them to the earth's other inhabitants. But you learn something very different from horses who are born wild; and if they're any good, they keep that wildness throughout their lives to one degree or another. Chink's has, shall we say, a glint, a quality of that un-lost wildness.

She also had from the beginning a rather aristocratic self-esteem. Pat got his first look at this when he hired what he called "this little old hippie town kid" to feed for him. He cautioned the boy to feed Chink's first. The boy ignored the advice and was soon back in the house in panic to announce that Chink's was dying. Chink's was fine; she was simply so offended at not being fed first that she hurled herself on the ground and held her breath until she was given her grain.

In the beginning, Pat had a good cowboy named Windy Spurgeon working for him; and between Pat and Windy there was a lot of plain ranch riding to be done. So instead of keeping Chink's in a pen and riding her in an arena, they rode her out hard, day after day, for six weeks. She accumulated wet saddle blankets and lived on ordinary rations. She was getting treated like a cow horse, working cattle under the cliffs of the Cimarron, down along the quicksand on the North Canadian, in the brush, in the heat, and by the lonely windmills that are the principal monuments of the panhandle. Chink's thrived on it and began to show a sense of purpose that rekindled Pat's hopes of her settling down as a cutting horse.

It was time to prove it; Pat set out for the El Paso Coliseum, home of a prestigious stock show cutting. It is necessary to understand the atmosphere at one of these important cuttings to understand what Chink's did. They have often been compared to funerals for their near silence; for unlucky riders, the muffled steps of their horses' feet on the coliseum floor sound like a cortege. But all is decorous, the judge in his place, pencil poised, ready to mark your horse down for losing a cow, leaking out from the herd too far, slinging his rear in his turns instead of cracking over his hocks, or just standing up too straight. The herd holders are in solemn attendance, the turn-back men poised facing the herd.

At the El Paso show, Chink's was tied along the fence under saddle, a safe distance from the cutting. For some reason, she broke her reins and went on a high-speed tour of the coliseum. In the words of Jerry Mills, another competitor, "A black beast was loose." She ran through the middle of the cutting and reduced it to chaos. Pat Jacobs watched this from the bleachers, eating a bag of popcorn. Finally, a large group of people circled the mare in the middle of the arena and contained her. Pat came down from the grandstand and pushed through the crowd, which was trying to identify the horse. "That's Jerry Mills's horse," said Pat.

When the cutting resumed, Pat barricaded Chink's in a roping box. She fixed him: splinters. Then she tried to leap out of the coliseum, high-centering on the sides; and finally she succeeded. The first description I ever had of Chink's Benjibaby was that she was the horse that jumped out of El Paso Coliseum.

I finally saw Chink's perform at Longmont, Colorado. Pat's stallion was getting a rest from the road. Rosie, Andy, and Wade, the Jacobses' three smart children, now grown with children of their own, were all showing cutting horses. So, of course, were Nellie and Pat. Pat knew of my fascination with Chink's and he led the mare up to me. It was inside a barn at night and the horse is gleaming black. She's not terribly big; but she has a narrow, beautiful head and a kind, if slightly possessed, look in her eyes. I was tired from traveling and I just stared at her. "Tom," said Pat, "here's Chink's Benjibaby."

When Pat showed her the next day, I knew what she could do. She turned around with cattle so quickly that it looked like an optical illusion. And the angle of her body to the ground was so drastic I couldn't see how she ever regained her balance. In fact, she never slipped a foot. I knew from Pat she thrived on impossible conditions like deep mud or slippery hardpan. And she hunted cattle like a cat, deliberately overshooting on her turns, stopping, and watching out of the corner of her eye for the last split second before running, sinking into her dying stop, and catching them up. When the cattle wouldn't try her, she sometimes jumped up and down in frustration.

Cutting is ruled by its judges; and its judges are ruled by the fashions of cutting or, shall we say, prevailing opinion. It's not like racing, where the first horse over the line wins. Human judgment as to what constitutes a great horse and a great ride will always spell the difference. But some judges are too sorry to assess the bravery of reckless horses like Chink's, and so they become all-or-nothing horses; because, with judges as with other men, there are none so blind as those who will not see. Nevertheless, as Pat began to go to cuttings, it soon became clear that Chink's Benjibaby could finish last at a cutting and be the only horse anyone remembered. Horses like that pit the fans against the judges; they change the history of cutting. At a recent finals of the National Cutting Horse Association Futurity at Will Rogers coliseum in Fort Worth, I sat in a sold-out crowd of people who were booing all five of the cautious judges for being so caught up in their rule books they were unable to see the run everyone else had seen. The judges at the futurity had never been through this before. They looked around in panic as though this could end up getting life-threatening. I thought it was good for them.

Trying to find out more about Chink's in the atmosphere of the Jacobs household was not easy. Something was always going on. The youngest boy, Wade, sat around reading *The Art of Deer Hunting,* then got up the next morning and bagged a record-class buck. Andy went to endless basketball practices, conferred with his coach, considered a college scholarship, and fed horses when Wade wasn't feeding horses. Rosie practiced barrel racing, needled me, helped her mother, and remarked there would be good cutting-horse judges when the judges quit reading cutting-horse magazines. Nellie's mother, Minnie, who'd had eleven children and who had more energy in her seventies than the rest of us have at thirteen, cheated at cards, hid beer, cracked jokes, baked desserts, and, when Rosie tipped over her glass, cheerfully admonished, "Now you'll never be a virgin!" They all eat or sleep when they're hungry or tired. There is no schedule, and I guess the connection is this: after being sold every six months of her life, Chink's Benjibaby landed on a ranch where a horse who didn't do things by the book could be understood by people who didn't care who had rejected her.

Pat took me out and showed me some of the country Chink's ended up in: an old hangman's cottonwood, a place where a German sat all night long on a tractor seat affixed to a post, watching the stars rotate, acquiring enough information to paint the solar system all over the walls of his house. We visited Bill Spurgeon, Windy's brother, on his little ranch and talked about the great calf-roping horses he has trained. It seemed I kept meeting thoughtful, intelligent people with a lot of character in a part of the country widely considered Nowhere. "This is where the hoot owls make love to the chickens," says Pat.

I suppose that when Pat told me he never won a fight with Chink's, he meant in the parlance of that trade that he "got with" the horse as opposed to making a push-button horse, one you can control with your feet and hands at the expense of the horse's ability to think. He has a special opinion of King Benjiman's daughters as genius cow horses who will "fall off a cliff looking at a bird." But they have made-up minds in some ways, and you don't go rebuilding them. The reward is that about the time you figure them out, they figure you out. You have to get this close to cutting horses to do anything.

I think Pat has been sorely tested by Chink's. About the time he thought she was going to behave like other horses and join the twentieth century, Chink's stalked and attacked a derelict Model T Ford, striking it with her front feet and tearing out the upholstery with her teeth. Then she won a cutting going away.

For a great part of the West, outside the Southwest and California, the most important exhibition for cutting horses is the Denver Stock Show. Pat decided to take Chink's Benjibaby, gambling that what he saw in her would come out.

In front of a coliseum filled with thousands of spectators, some sophisticated about cutting and others knowing no more than that it was a man horseback working cattle in the rites of an old collaboration, Chink's left the lesson beyond doubt with her stunning turns and the sliding stops where her graceful body seemed to sink in front and behind all at once, drawing feints and moves out of cattle they might never have had on their own. A century ago in her present home on the panhandle, between the Cimarron and the North Canadian, Chink's and Pat might have helped one another sort cattle in the vast herds of that time. But today the roaring crowd, now standing on the bleachers and shouting, prevented Pat from even hearing the signal that his run was over. People walked toward them across the arena to tell him that the time was up. But Pat and the crazy mare were head to head with a single cow, absolutely alone in an old dance.

A cowboy's horse had come home.

7
ROANIE

There is a notion that you get only one great horse in a lifetime, a persistent notion that I hope isn't true; because, if that is the case, I've already had mine, in fact still have him though he is an arthritic old man twenty-six years old. His name is Lucky Bottom 79 and he was already a terrific horse when I acquired him over twenty years ago, though for some reason, he wasn't doing much and had a reputation for being a bronc that had probably kept someone else from buying him. He is called Roanie for his red roan coat, a coat that turns almost purple in the summer, and he is not a very pretty horse. In fact, he won an informal contest one year in Hamilton for being the ugliest horse in Montana. He has a slight Roman nose, actually called the "Burt bump" for a trait inherited from his grandsire Burt. As to the length of his head, it's been remarked that he can drink from a fifty-gallon drum and still keep an eye on you. His sire was a good horse called Lucky Star Mac, an Oklahoma Star–bred horse; and his mother was a racehorse named Miss Glimpse. Roanie is one of those hotheaded horses about which people say, "The only safe place is on his back." He can kick in any direction, has actually stripped the buttons off the front of a man's shirt, and the extreme suspicion that is continuously in his eye doesn't come from nowhere. Roanie was not the sort of horse Buster prefers but he once said to me, "Boy, when he was on, that roan horse was unbelievable!"

Lucky Bottom 79 was trained by a part-Cherokee cowboy named Ed Bottom, who is, any way you look at it, an outstanding horseman who has made an everlasting mark training calf-roping and cutting horses for nearly half a century. Like Buster Welch, Ed is a member of the Cutting Horse Hall of Fame. Yesterday, I tried to catch swaybacked old Roanie in a twenty-foot loafing shed. He went by me like mercury, low, quick, and throwing me such an elegant head fake I'm lucky I didn't fall down.

Ed Bottom lives in Asher, Oklahoma, next door to the Barrow farm, former home of Clyde Barrow. One of Ed's childhood heroes was a family friend, Pretty Boy Floyd, and Ed remembers Pretty Boy coming home from robberies, hiding his shot-up Hudson in a sheep shed, giving all the kids silver dollars, and pitching horseshoes with the grown-ups.

I traveled to Oklahoma to try Roanie and I remember two things distinctly. When I went out to the corral to saddle and work a cow on him, Mrs. Bottom said, "Don't fall off."

Responding to this nicety, I said, "I won't."

Mrs. Bottom said, "You won't?"

I had some time to think about this as we got Roanie ready. Roanie hadn't seen me before and I have never been around a horse that exuded such all-consuming distrust of strangers. However, once I was on his back and loping in a circle all was well, with the exception of one small thing: the horse kept his head turned so that he could look back and watch me the whole while.

I cut the first cow on him. The cow stopped, looked, prepared for sudden motion, and Roanie began to sink. I guess you would call it a crouch. But it was level all around and I simply sensed the ground coming up: this horse had a working altitude of about a man's waist and I soon found that he had real speed and the ability to turn right through himself like a dishrag. And he understood cattle. He could mesmerize them or stop them with sheer speed, all at hot-rod roadster height. And as I would learn over the years, either his sense of play or his sense of rightness in the world made him purely at home only when he was working cattle. At such a time, you couldn't spur him or misride him to the wrong spot with the strength of Superman. He knew with certainty where he wanted to be and the door to the suggestion box was nailed shut. Over the years, several outstanding cutting-horse riders have competed on him without success. Evidently, he disliked all their opinions and convictions. I was too ignorant and perhaps intimidated by him to let him do anything but what he wanted to do. That proved to be the right approach. For a few years, I made more money on his back than I did at my actual job. It was a great feeling to know you were probably going to win a cutting before you even unloaded the horse from the trailer.

I bought Roanie on the condition he pass a veterinary exam. We took him to the local vet and after Roanie kicked the X-ray plates all over the building and took a couple of shots at the X-ray machine itself, we decided to forgo the exam and accept instead Ed's statement, "You can't hurt him with an axe handle." The demoralized veterinarian was reduced to inquiring rhetorically, "Why do you people always want to X-ray everything?" Ed gave me two bits made by another Cherokee, John Israel, identical except for the length of the shanks and beautifully fashioned from salvaged old hay rakes. "Tune him in the long shanks and show him in the short ones." That was the end of the operating instructions. We headed home.

It was early spring on the ranch, snowy and muddy. A friend of mine stopped by to see Roanie and the muck sucked his overshoe off in the corral. He looked at the slush filling the boot as he stood in his stocking foot. "There it is," he said, "ag world." I led Roanie around, then put him in a box stall to protect him from the change of Montana weather and settled in to start building a relationship with him.

Roanie had not always done well in box stalls. At the national futurity for three-year-olds, he had a record-setting run that brought the audience to its feet. Afterward, Ed put him in one of the assigned box stalls. Someone had placed a blanket in the stall that Roanie had never seen before. By the time Roanie spotted it, his friend Ed was back in the bleachers and Roanie felt he had little choice but to kick the door, its latch and hinges, off the box stall and race out in equine hysteria to scatter spectators. Ed was summoned on the loudspeaker and things were soon put right. If there was a big problem, it was lost on Ed, who is the last word in coolheaded. His comment on Roanie's escapade: "I guess he didn't want to be in there."

I didn't know that story at the time I got Roanie home. All I know is that when I went into the box stall with him, he flattened himself against the wall in terror and when I moved, he began to whirl. It was like the end of *Little Black Sambo*, where all the tigers turn into a pool of butter, only I didn't want to be in that pool. Sharing a tiny room with an eleven-hundred-and-fifty-pound whirling panicked animal is a situation that impresses one with its gravity. I had to do something. The check hadn't cleared yet and I could hardly confine our relationship to watching him through the window. This was not a public aquarium.

The next day, I moved a small school desk into Roanie's stall. Then I went in and sat down and did my work. For the first hour, Roanie seemed to be trying to smear himself into the plank walls. He trembled from head to toe. At the end of the hour, I was still writing and he was getting tired of his exertions. He was standing with his weight equally distributed on all four feet. When I got up to pet him, he flattened himself once more. I found myself, pen in hand, seated at my desk, hunched over a legal pad, making such plaintive cries as, "Roanie, I gotta take a leak!" In three days, he was tired of my writing life, trying to figure out how to get around the desk to the hay. We'd made a start.

We began riding out on the ranch. This he adored: new country. It was always a special pleasure to simply use him as a saddle horse because he was the sort of horse that always seemed to pull you through the country, head stretched forward, ears pricked, drinking up the new space. There is nothing quite like looking over wild land from horseback.

I don't know how Roanie would have done in battle though I think once he'd gotten the idea of what the job was, he would have excelled. His panic attacks, however, would have been dangerous to friend and foe alike. Early in my ownership of him, his feet, accustomed to red Oklahoma dirt, got sore on the rocks where I live. Finally, he went quite lame. It turned out to be merely a stone bruise but a shadow on his X-rays suggested a fractured coffin bone. I sent him immediately to Colorado State University's outstanding equine veterinary center in Fort Collins and called the excellent lameness specialist there. I explained to this specialist that Roanie could be quite unpredictable; to avoid having people getting hurt, I urged caution.

"Mr. McGuane, we are well accustomed to handling horses of all kinds. Owners often give us these sorts of warnings and, while we think it is considerate, we don't worry about it too much." The doctor, a cultivated Australian, took me for a nervous sort.

Within a few days, he called me. His voice was elevated in both pitch and intensity. "Your horse is going to get this university sued back to the stone age! I have had to rescue several of my graduate students from him and I have hung a skull and crossbones on his stall!" They had tranquilized my horse from the sort of range usually considered appropriate for the rhinoceros and managed to examine him enough to conclude that his hoof injury wasn't serious. When his health papers came back with him, a notation read, "Lucky Bottom 79's rectal temperature not taken as he continually endangered human life."

"I'd like a photograph of someone riding this horse," were the doctor's last words to me.

"The only safe place is on his back," I said but I think it fell on deaf ears.

In any case, he was soon sound once again and in glistening physical condition. We worked cattle at home and he was quick and smooth. I decided to take him to a cutting-horse contest in Blackfoot, Idaho, on the weekend. I knew I had a special horse.

The cutting was held in a city park right in the middle of town. It seemed kind of odd not to have a lot of open country around us but the cattle had been, in the words of Chuck Tyson, a great old cow man, "surrounded by cleverness" and things were rather orderly. Roanie had not been to a cutting in a good while and, as I was to learn, he knew the difference between a cow in a contest and a cow anywhere else. As soon as I unloaded him and he heard the bawling cattle and saw the spectators, his blood began to boil. I tried to gallop him down but he just got crazier. I decided to walk him and keep him calm. He gaped around at everything, froze, and shied from paper cups, cigarette wrappers, the light off windshields; children who'd never seen a horse flare its nostrils, snort, and run backward from a gum wrapper gathered around and made my composure worse with their astonished questions. "Hey mister, what's the matter with your horse?" Or, "He's loco, ain't he?" I consoled myself by knowing that as soon as I rode him into the herd, everything would settle down and the eternal cow-horse logic would take over. Boldly, I entered both the open and the non-professional classes.

I had an excellent draw in the open. I hired my herd holders and turn-back man and rode confidently toward the herd. I thought Roanie's walk was uncustomarily jerky but gave it little thought as we turned through the cattle and began to drive out. A pretty baldface heifer slipped up onto the point of the herd and I eased forward, cut her, and put my rein hand down on Roanie's neck. Roanie stood bolt upright, the perfect position, I thought, for him to jump out of his skin. He looked bug-eyed at the cow until she moved and then he reared up on his hind legs, pawing the air like Roy Rogers's Trigger on LSD, and with several huge kangaroo leaps shot past the turn-back horses, blowing snot in two directions, and bolted into the Blackfoot city park, scattering strollers and people of all ages. When I got him stopped, I turned to look back at the cutting-horse contest. All I could see was a wall of blank faces. The judge gave me a zero because he was unaware of a lower number.

I decided that the only way around this was through it and so I did not scratch from the next class; and I was only mildly unnerved by the voices I heard as I rode toward the cattle: "He's not going in there *again,* is he?" In the crowd were some unmitigated gawkers of the kind that swarm to accident scenes. I cut two cows in the course of my run and Roanie laid down a performance that was absolutely faultless. We won the cutting by a serious margin. It seemed to be that we had gotten through something together because I became abruptly more sensitive to the world as he saw it. I used to think that when I led him out of his box stall at a cutting I could tell by the look in his eye if he was going to win it that day. If he seemed to gaze upon the world with easy vigilance, I knew that we would be deep in the money. If the look of incomplete understanding was there, if he fixated on a bucket or a snakelike curve of garden hose, I knew we would have to find some way to cool out before we began, often by a ride around the neighborhood or, if we were at a local Montana cutting, a visit to one of his horse friends at another trailer. In any case, from then on the pressure was on me to cut my cows correctly and to ride him well; in doing such a tremendous job of holding up his end, he gave me much room for error. I tried not to abuse it.

I felt so competitive when I was riding this horse that I went to every last little cutting in the region and got a wonderful education in the geography of the Northern Rockies, so many little towns in which the fairgrounds were the only public gathering place. It's been more than a decade since I rode him in a contest but people still inquire about him everywhere I go. "How's the old roan horse?" they ask, shaking their heads in awe. It's so nice to tell them he's fine, and free, in a big grassy place. Not that I don't sometimes wish it were long ago and I were throwing a saddle up on his powerful withers with the feeling that I could hardly wait for my draw.

8
ON THE ROAD AGAIN

It was a uniquely brutal December in Montana. In my haystack, spaces between bales were filled with dead songbirds, a whole flight that missed the southern migration in an early storm. Our driveway drifted in with snow on a daily basis. On our front porch a wind chime hangs, audible throughout the kitchen and generally pleasant. It became more active in December but by January it sounded like Lionel Hampton on crank.

We caught a ride for four of our horses to California and began to scheme about getting warm. For another month, they basked while we fought the good fight and paid their board by U.S. Mail. We wanted to join them.

Wallace Stegner said to me once, "You're an animal man, aren't you?"

"Yes," I said proudly, "I'm an animal man." There are lots of us animal people, including those of us who when young were driven obsessively to pet shops. Our family has come together from the animal-filled households of many families. Dogs, cats, birds, and we've doggedly watched dreadful TV animal shows with hosts in safari coats. We animal people are most fond of Edward O. Wilson because in his science we can still smell the origins of an animal nut able to expend infinite human love on ants. I have never been able to get enough animal, never close enough to my dogs. I would not have fallen for horses to the degree I have if I could ride my dogs: you go with what you've got. But compared to a dog, a horse is a sphinx. Horses reward familiarity with acceptance, a stirring thing from an animal that is not born tame. Raised with horses, our dogs wander freely among their legs without mishap; and at feeding time, the dogs all enjoy a few collegial flakes of alfalfa. A dog could make a fine attorney, but never a horse. Dogs seem to think of horses as bumpkins. There is little salesmanship in the horse.

When we've traveled with our horses, we have often been uncomfortable leaving them at unattended rodeo grounds while we hunted up a motel, then sleeping but lightly while we imagined the now universal hooligans, letting them out, throwing firecrackers into their stalls or stealing them—all things we've heard of happening. Various companies who make trailers have learned how to supply the needs of worriers like my wife and me. They build horse trailers with compact living quarters in them, for the humans. Our children, who see a risible connection to the world of RVs, have, after the Winnebago, dubbed ours the Horseabago. My friend, Jim Harrison, whom we will visit in the present narrative, is more thoughtfully reminded of the French farmhouse wherein folk and livestock are separated by a wall thinner than those at the Super 8. We simply pictured ourselves in one end, Delta, Sassy, Zip, and Lina in the other, and wheels underneath.

We wrote the check and drove off with our Labrador Shelagh to take delivery in central California, then set out for home by the Great Circle Route to take in some cuttings and see some country—towing four horses, four saddles, ten bridles, eight saddle blankets, three breast collars, shoeing tools, equine pharmaceuticals, alfalfa, timothy hay, water buckets, brushes, hoof picks, slickers, boots, clothes, a toilet, a shower, a stove, a microwave, a refrigerator, a bed, a table, an awning, a sink, and a color TV. It was a modern farm at seventy-five miles per hour. To calm my nerves crossing the cities of southern California bound for the cutting at Temecula, I listened to Arnold Weinstein's lectures on the classics of American literature on audiotape. My wife, Laurie, suggested at one point that this implied a two-track existence between the cultivated and the moronic, and that sooner or later we would have to choose. *Faw!* as the old fur trappers once exclaimed, when faced with sibylline conundra. The real test, as far as I was concerned, lay not in our capacity for withstanding incongruities like cutting-horse contests in southern California, but rather in our ability, after a quarter century of living on the wide prairie—sometimes just wide enough for our prickly dispositions—to reduce our playing field to what Barbara Streisand would reject as a shoe closet. We would see: weeks of aluminum-bound intimacy lay ahead.

We began by renting a small farmhouse for a few weeks near Los Olivos, California, where we shared a yard and driveway with a nice woman named Concha and her large family. It was the month of January and we had stolen guiltily from our home in Montana. If you leave Montana for so much as one day in January, the neighbors will greet you on return with, "Back for the summer?" It's barely worth it. The atmosphere was California agricultural, with an eager rooster who climbed onto a 1974 Oldsmobile Toronado engine block and announced the day an hour before dawn right below our bedroom window. My horse Zip injured a suspensory tendon, and we were trying to get him treated if not rehabilitated before we left to go cutting. Each day we went to Dave MacGregor's place and worked all four of our horses. Much of central California is still farming country. Where we were staying has been given over increasingly to grapes. It is a mixed blessing. The grape arborists have bulldozed thousands of the old and beautiful oaks, finally bringing upon themselves a wave of serious indignation. Planting, pruning, and harvesting grapes are done by gangs of workers who are made to appear at opportune times, then to disappear at the end of the job. When you pass these California farm fields, there are, at specific intervals of time, small gangs of migrant workers, their old cars parked along the road. The lunch boxes and yellow raincoats are usually organized in one spot while these durable stoop workers lend their valuable if temporary skills. Americans are no longer willing to gather their own food.

Early in the morning, when I fed my horses, I sometimes surprised wild pigs retreating under the palest blue sky. The horses were gathered under a gothic oak with a full moon in its branches. Sticking out of the adobe soil were old cow skulls from Spanish days. I saw my neighbors getting ready for work in the fields, chattering in Spanish, while their children waited for the school bus, chattering in English. A century and a half ago, the Anglos pushed the Spanish out of California. Now they're back, concealed in the skin of the surviving Indians. Frantic local politicians, aging surfers, born-again Christians, English-only advocates, affluent climate buffs describe the assault of immigrants on the "infrastructure" with the fervor of those being pushed into the sea. Armed with a personal view of U.S. history, they viewed gene mapping as a black art. The old mission at San Miguel Arcangel, built by European priests with Indian slaves, is a parish church for their mestizo descendants. Possession, says an old saw, is nine tenths of the law.

A few miles below my bucolic surroundings was another local phenomenon: Route 101, six lanes of screaming metal. How they can coexist is one of many California mysteries, like the emptiness of the Carizzo Plains, the Pacific Ocean, the devouring megapolitan crawl.

In my rented farmhouse, I built courage to take on the L.A. Freeway in my pickup truck and thirty-eight foot horse trailer. I found an old family album belonging to the man who surveyed the Channel Islands in the last century. There were pictures of the survey-ors' first business in ramshackle Rocky Mountain mine camps, boom towns that have gone back to desert, spidery bridges being built over the Santa Ynez river, a horse-drawn black hearse. I had several trips to the local radiator shop to install an auxiliary fuel tank and there I met an old farmer who lived on the banks of the Santa Ynez, where, in his youth, twenty-eight thousand steelhead ran. They caught them on rods, they caught them on chicken wire, they caught them when they ran up on the beach at the lit-tle town of Surf in their assault on the estuary. The fish came all winter; and in March came a race of short thick steelhead they called silversides. Then the State of California punched a hole in the mountain, filled up a phony lake, and sent the water the other way, to Santa Barbara. The steelhead have vanished. Not even British Columbia or Alaska have a run like the Santa Ynez had. Another California gone. The question is, how many are left?

After three weeks, I was emotionally tuned up for my trip. I had watched the semitrucks with new admiration. Laurie had prepared for the trip by buying a sparkling blue cell phone with which to stay in touch with everyone. And I had promised that there would be no road rage, a tall order in a state where car dueling is a way of life. Proper use of a turn signal only triggers Californians to cut you off. You must make your move instantly after signaling or they've got you, your reaction time against theirs. Only one law prevails on the California highway, and it is the law of the sucker punch.

The day of departure arrived and we loaded our four horses and increasingly worried dog in the dark. We even beat the neighbor's chicken. The coyotes had got into the grape arbors and kept us awake with their singing. We were ready to go. We had everything with us and were prepared for travel in all weathers. At the moment, it looked like rain. I managed the driveway without mishap, though we required both lanes of the road we pulled out on. The various running lights on the trailer streaming behind me gave me a vague Casey Jones feeling as I started down our long canyon toward the freeway eight miles away. When we reached it, traffic was still moderate and I was able to pull on and get up to speed and take my place modestly in the slow lane. Laurie was doing preliminary map work for the blizzard of interchanges that faced us some hours down the road. Betweentimes, she read the instruction manual for her cell phone.

As we drove along the ocean, the sun began to come up. Passing Point Conception, which lies seaward of the highway, gives the impression of an oak-filled expanse of ranch land that extends to the sea without interruption. After the racehorse farms, we passed vast citrus groves with what appeared to be this year's harvest rotting on the ground. Spinning along in the semi-dark with us were the laborers in their jalopies hurrying to pick the food and clean up the messes. The favored machine is a stylishly designed and utterly used-up compact car whose pert styling contrasts morbidly with its current dilapidation. These are often covertly on the highway, having flunked the California emissions test. It is all their occupants can do to keep California from collapsing. But there we were, all heading south, a thousand different missions and obligations, and the urgency of the highway was building fast.

And then we were crossing Los Angeles, part of an infinitely complex symphony of traffic. I found myself, as I always do when driving for long in California, becoming caught up in the local obsession with the automobile. As we passed car lots, I tried to spot sexy new models, despite that I was hurtling along with a load of hay and horses. "There's the new BMW roadster," I cried out to my wife, who was fixated in sensible terror over her map. But I was picturing the wind in my hair, bucket seats, the beach. I was recalling happier days of hot-rod obsession, Deuce roadsters, flathead Fords, magical names like Edelbrock and Iskinderian, speed tuners from deep in my car-crazed memory. Oncoming traffic was pouring into my flanks from either side until I was part of a southbound general river of metal, confined in four directions to the gestalt of a seventy-two-mile-an-hour traffic jam. It was impossible to know where to place myself. If I picked what I thought was the slow lane, it either turned into a bombardment of oncoming traffic or, worse, it became a nearly inescapable exit lane taking you to Pomona or Palm Springs. Since I could not imagine being swept onto one of these off-ramps with any hope of return, I hit the turn signal and forced my way back onto a through lane in a cascade of indignant horn blowing. Most would finally yield, but I soon learned to spot the goatees and backward hats of the demented drivers who would rather force their cars into one of the horse stalls than let me back into their lanes. No form of road rage short of magnum goose loads through their windshields seemed adequate; so, I became successfully oblivious, though my peculiar mind music contained the sonorous cough of the Benelli Super Black Magnum ten-gauge waterfowler. I marveled at all the time that had passed since the Eagles' "L.A. Freeway." The melancholy druggers of those period lyrics seemed straight out of *Brigadoon* compared to the zombies currently overflowing southern Californian pavement.

The intermittent dividing lines of the lanes flowed at me ominously. Sometimes I looked into my rearview mirror and saw only giant letters, KENILWORTH or FRUEHOFF. I remembered trying, years ago, to write a song with my brother-in-law and quitting after the line "She had eyes like the headlights of a Fruehoff coming at you in the night." Nice meter but lacking in the seductive atmosphere to which we aspired.

At length, we made it to Route 15, bound for San Diego and its environs, including Chula Vista, locally known as Chulajuana, where a local heart transplant recipient was found to have not a defective heart but a colossal mandrake root, which was sold by the hospital to local sorcerers who buried it in desert near Borrego Springs to ward off a subdivision. That year more real-estate deals failed to clear escrow than any in history since the time of the De Anza expedition three hundred years ago. In a most famous instance, an upscale retirement community rapidly devolved into an open-pit borax mine employing licensed but temporarily indisposed realtors.

We planned to stop well short of Chulajuana, in Temecula, a dizzily evolving small, western-looking town that is sending out malls and planned hamlets in all directions, up and down the hills into the special California great beyond. A couple of years ago, we admired a new town surrounding a broad, gentle lake; but this year when we passed, the lake was gone. "Where's that lake?!" Laurie shouted intemperately. As a child of Old Alabama, she is furious at all this moving about of the landscape and is weirdly fixated on natural features "staying put."

I was still occupied with the real business of being here, playing it as it lays at three thousand RPMs. I had one off-ramp to conquer and a hard left. Laurie was fiddling madly with her cell phone, which had numerous tiny buttons, unparalleled range, more memory than any of our children, and palm-snuggling ergonomics. She had started our trip by buying bulk-rate airtime, which seemed to reinforce the sense that we were falling off the end of the earth. Not much had happened with it so far, though I'd heard her cry, "I can't get any reception!" a few times, after our speculations as to whether various of the kids had "gotten there yet," or "heard about that job." The little phone had so far only emphasized our distance, producing affectless recorded messages from a communications empire identified to us only by its acronym. I rather thought that KGB, ATT, CIA, ITT, and so on had begun running together.

The light was out at the bottom of the off-ramp. In its place was a well-groomed police officer, directing traffic. I stopped and awaited his directions. When he noticed me, he furiously signaled me with angry gestures to make my turn as though I should have known what to do in the first place. I rolled down my window as we passed him and said that I was waiting for him to signal me. "*Fuck you!*" shouted the California police officer. I imagined being a brownskinned food gatherer pulled from the trunk of an unregistered jalopy by this turkey and my blood ran cold.

We made it to the fine and expansive DL ranch, where the cutting was to be held. I felt liberated to have so much wiggle room for my big rig. I swung around in a circle, cut it too tight, and managed to burst the back window of my truck with the corner of the trailer with a big noise and in full view of everyone. "I'll never live this down," I commented to a cutter from northern California. "No," he said, "until someone else screws up, you're 'the trailer guy.'" As with others of my kind, I knew immediately in my mind's eye where the duct tape was. We picked a nice place to set up our camp. I had never before felt the bounty of water and electricity hookups. Laurie and I sometimes fuss at each other about where to park, and parking your rolling home makes the selection one of a home site. Here one must form a principle along the lines of you're doing the best you can. I know there are no trees but there's water. The world of rolling homes is oddly genderless, though the boys who are mechanically inclined try to isolate themselves on an RV Olympus with specialized information about things you can't see, like the insides of motors. In real RV clusters, there is often a soothsayer who treats the big rigs with a laying on of hands and sacerdotal murmuring: "Bleed the hydraulics now or you'll never get 'er stopped." "She's losing everything through the intercooler." "They're all squirrelly at seven thousand feet." And so on.

Laurie plunged in with her usual energy and between us we unloaded horses, fed and watered them, hooked up power and water, jacked the trailer, and released the truck. It began to rain and soon we were tucked away in the trailer, supper cooking, operation manuals for water pumps, holding tanks, hot-water heaters, microwave ovens, propane tanks, and generators spread out on the dinette table. The rain drummed down.

When we fed our four horses early the next morning, I noted all the horses and trailers that had arrived while we slept. There were hundreds of cutting horses, heads sticking out of stall doors, impatient for breakfast. People stumbled in from the rain underneath the shed roofs wearing boots whose weight had doubled with the masses of mud and a local gumbo called "D.G.," for deteriorated granite, a substance that abrades and ruins shoes in record time. While the horses ate, Laurie and I had a look at the cattle, which were penned about a quarter mile away. They were light, fast-looking brahma cattle with a lot of ear. We would have to be on our toes to manage these little rockets. You can pretty much tell which latitude you're on in the American West by looking at the cattle. Far enough south and they will be dewlapped, downeared; and as you head north, the dewlaps disappear, the ears shorten and angle increasingly upward. Finally, at my parallel, the forty-fifth, you see the customary easygoing English cattle—Angus and Hereford—with a sprinkling of exotics like Charolais, Simmental, and . . . you back there, Bouviers de Flandres is a dog, not a cow.

Jimmy Kemp, a cutter from Brady, Texas, who has been cooking for masses of friends at contests all winter, stuck his hand into the rain and said, "This might be a good night for chili." No one knows what gustatory windfalls might occur at Kemptown, which is Jimmy's trailer and appurtenances, including a huge propane-fired barbecue and a prep table. Times past have included crawfish étouffée for forty, several dozen wild quail cooked over coals, fresh asparagus, new potatoes, portabello mushrooms, big bacon-wrapped Gulf shrimp, and aged steaks. He rides a smart gelding he calls Einstein, pronounced "Ahnstahn." We all hope Einstein takes Jimmy to plenty of pay windows so he can invest it in food. Jimmy Kemp must be an optimist because I have loped circles with him at daybreak on our horses and listened to him plan the evening menu.

I was already nervous because I had never competed on my horse Lena before. My usual mount, Zippy, had been lame for a year and it seemed I had talked about nothing but lameness in horses that entire time, hock problems in hard stoppers like Zip, stifle injuries, caudal pain, splints, stifles, sweenies. I'd tried everything, radiography, bone scans, cortisone injections, isoxsuprine, butazolidin, break-over aluminum shoes, chiropractors, masseuses, and magnets! But he healed very slowly.

So, I bought a nice young mare from Jan and Jerry Bob Seago in Oklahoma, beautifully trained by Jerry Bob. When I went down to try her, I got completely lost in the various animal-based interests of the Seagos and nearly forgot why I was there. There were longhorned cattle wandering around the yards, numerous cowdogs, twenty or thirty horses, yearling cattle, and in an extended yard an enthralling breeding operation for fighting cocks. Each of these beautiful birds was tethered in front of a small shelter. Jerry Bob picked them up one at a time. The roosters allowed themselves to be turned on their backs while Jerry Bob recited their lineage. One was a Kelso, another a Doc Robinson, another a greenleg, and so on. Behind us was the roost and incubator where the more modest hens conveyed their warlike genetics to the innocuous eggs, which, though suitable for any farm breakfast, produced these heroic birds. Jerry Bob praised them, "This one here's *mean* to chickens." Or, holding aloft a princely rooster of five vivid colors, huge feet sticking out before him, "Chicken turn his back on this guy, he's dead." Or, with a passionate gleam in his eye, "Now here's one likes to spar!" Since their metal spurs were not attached to them, Jerry Bob could safely toss a couple of these boys together for some training. The roosters bounced around before each other, neck feathers flared impressively, making thrilling strategic feints and moves before Jerry Bob swooped in and caught them up to return them to their tethers. Presently he looked off and said, "I like coming down here, get away from them Goddamn horses." He said it with the same fatalism he had used when he gestured around at his place happily and said, "What can I say, we're Okies." I've never had a bad time in Oklahoma, which is like a Midwestern version of Texas, or Texas without the attitude. Texans seem proud of their reticence; Oklahomans talk all the time. It is an unguarded, countrified place, marvelously lacking in self-consciousness.

Looking around at my rather complete rolling home, I considered the example of my friend Don, a single man who rides cutting horses. He enjoys meeting women on his trips and has often said to me that the key is having a good cooler. He keeps his Igloo filled with sophisticated snacks, Black Diamond cheddar, Fuji apples, a crisp Traminer, refreshing lagers, sourdough baguettes, alder-smoked chicken or turkey or ham, red onions, lovely Norwegian sardines. "You run a good cooler," says Don, "and you won't be able to keep them off with a stick." I was not in a position to try to overpower Don's cooler with my Horseabago, but I felt that it was in the air that I could if I had to.

Roger Peters and his wife, Lisa, old friends from Nebraska, pay us a visit at our trailer. Roger and I each owned a Lucky Bottom horse and they were two of the best, Roger's Lucky Bottom 18 and my Lucky Bottom 79. They were extremely snorty but talented horses that required infinite understanding. Roger had, at the time, an enterprise called "Peters' Wieners," in Nebraska, with the challenging motto "Nobody Beats Our Meat." Today, Roger and Lisa, after the usual pleasantries, had something they wanted to take up

with us and I sensed their reluctance to intrude. Finally Roger spoke: "I don't want to stick my nose in
where it doesn't belong, but I hope you are using RV-
recommended toilet paper." I assured him that we
were. "Because if you don't," Roger went on in a more
emboldened fashion, "your waste tank is going to be
the most ungodly wreck. I mean, you really don't want
to see what happens." This seemed to have been ac-
companied by the roll of kettle drums.

I had a terrible draw on Lena, dead last on wild cattle. I studied the herd trying to pick out some cattle
that I hoped wouldn't run me over. Someone recommended the brindle "mot" (short for motley faced,
also called "brockle face" or "brock"). There was a
nice redneck cow with a smeared brand I hoped no
one cut and a "race cow" that presented itself as
workable that you couldn't hold with a gun. In a herd
of seventy-five head, they tended to blur and late in
the draw it was like a swarm of bees in there. I rode in
and couldn't find any of my favorites. I cut a hard-
moving Brahma heifer who got right in Lena's face.
Lena stopped with such deep smoothness that we
were able to handle things at pretty high speed without getting beat. In the increasingly muddy conditions, she was sliding halfway past the cow but still
getting back to hold it. I got up over her too much and
really had to push off the saddle horn to stay where I
belonged. Laurie managed to have a respectable run

on Delta in ghastly conditions and we hung around to see if we might limp into the money. The rain increased and when Jimmy Kemp walked by, he held his hand out, palm upright to measure it and said, "This might be a good night for chili." Finally, the footing gave out and the announcer stated, "No sense crippling you or your horse," and called it off for the day.

We put our horses up and fed early. There was some difficulty getting hay and stall bedding delivered. A paint horse got loose and produced a wild circus atmosphere between the trailers. One disgusted cutter was trying to back out and leave, then recognized he was there for the duration.

We went into the living quarters of the trailer, left all the muddy clothes in the tack room and . . . got into our bathrobes! This seemed too good to be true. The rain beat down on the roof and Laurie was making hot chocolate on the stove. I stretched out on the couch and got so lost in a strange Brazilian novel that I forgot where I was until the cocoa arrived. Laurie stretched out in the opposite direction and we abandoned ourselves to lavishing admiration on our horses. I explained how pleased I had been with Lena's ability to bear down on wild cattle, watch them closely, and take care of work at hand. I added flourishes about her big eyes and graceful neck, her neat thoroughbred feet and long pasterns. I did note how she passed the loping horses without ever getting out of her smooth extended trot. And her stop! Montaigne said four hundred years ago, "There is nothing in which a horse's power is better revealed than in a neat, clean stop." Lena stops so deep I have to bell-boot her front feet to keep them from being hit by her back feet. Laurie listened to all of this patiently. She believes and I agree that her little mare Delta is the horse of her lifetime. Indeed, they have a fit together that seems to be working brilliantly. Delta is just a little over fourteen hands and has the personality of a Labrador who has always lived in the house. She follows Laurie around sleepily, checking her pockets for treats, sighs languidly when she's being saddled, seems too weary to be warmed up, and generally unable to decipher what all the excitement is about. Furthermore, she is afraid of cattle. But when Laurie cuts a cow out of the herd, something happens. The sleepy eyes turn into two hot coals and the inner Delta emerges, a blazing quick cow horse with so much style and precision that Laurie has the ongoing task of fending off importuning buyers.

I felt guilty about all my comfortable lying around the trailer and got up and dressed to water my horses. I stopped to talk to Don Boon, a serious competitor from Texas who rides a terrific gelding he calls Bullet. He was hauling buckets from his truck to his stalls. Bullet has enabled Don to win a tremendous amount of money despite Bullet's numerous leg ailments. One day, the young man who trained Bullet called Don and said he had another horse as good as Bullet. The owners wanted to sell him immediately and he was moderately priced. Don sent a check and the new horse was delivered. He was not as good as Bullet. Some months later, Don ran into the trainer, and a fine trainer he is, at a Texas cutting. "How'd you like to show Bullet in the open?" Don asked. The trainer was thrilled. He showed him and won the open. Later, when the two sat in the stands, the trainer asked Don, "How is it you decided to let me show Bullet?" "I let you show Bullet," said Don, "so that the next time you call me and tell me you got a horse just like Bullet you'll know what you're talking about." Interestingly, this was not told as a reproachful tale but rather as something more good-natured, in the manner of a card player describing how he guessed someone else's hand.

By the end of the Temecula cuttings, we were emerging from our winter rust and beginning to move at the same speed as the horses under us. The coefficient of drag was on the decline. We would soon be departing and there were details of housekeeping, which I, as co-owner of a rolling home, would have to attend to. I decided to work with the sewage and wastewater outlets. I use these two terms advisedly because at the outset I didn't quite know the difference between the two. My feeling that sewage versus wastewater was a matter of splitting hairs proved ill-directed. They are also known as gray water and black water. The outlets for these, consisting of capped pipes and knife valves, are under one side of the trailer and to get a feel for them, you need to crawl under there on your back and have a real good look. That is what I did. Once in viewing range, I noted that one knife valve was out and one was in. I thought to push the out valve in but it wouldn't budge. Am I understanding this? I wondered, letting my mind wander between "black," "gray," "sewage," and "waste," not to mention the combinations implied by caps and valves. Perhaps I should pull the in valve out; it seemed a logical thing to do. Laurie heard me cry out a complex phrase that was not "Great Caesar's Ghost!" When she asked for a real explanation, I shouted, "I'm covered with shit!" By then I'd stemmed the tide by pushing the in valve *back* in and was staggering around, shocked into an apelike crouch, trying to think of someone or something to blame.

We bade goodbye to our California friends as they banqueted that night at Roger Peters's trailer. Jimmy Kemp, unable to be merely a guest, arrived with superior bratwurst he had precooked in beer to be finished on the charcoal grill. We pulled our big rig east toward Indio and Lancaster and Blythe, a real no-man's-land of battered and forlorn desert, hopeful groves of palms encircling vanished buildings, assaultive high-yield farming faced off over available water with brand new towns, incongruous golf courses, "Fantasy Springs," a wilderness of wind generators—the kind of landscape I associate with space landings and Captain Beefheart (may he rest in peace). The traffic streams from L.A. to Phoenix past prison off-ramps with huge signs urging you not to pick up hitchhikers, antediluvian tractor-trailer rigs with tall shrouded stacks, rocketing luxury cars threading their way through the unlucky jalopies. You quickly take on the local travel mood: that you are fleeing.

At the end of the day, we found a place to rent four stalls where we could park our trailer. The owner, in pajama bottoms and T-shirt that read "Heavenly Bodies" and depicted vintage fifties hotrods across the expanse of his vast belly, walked past us without eye contact, tossed four flakes into the stalls and said, "Sixty dollars." Then he added that it would be all right if we wanted to turn our ponies into the roping arena for exercise, adding mirthlessly, "That's fifty, ha ha." He and his neighbor, he explained, are very strict about their property lines and have piled their tree trimmings and other moderately obnoxious debris between each other to emphasize that fact. Later, the two big bellies began shouting at each other across the property line, inciting tiny dogs invisible behind concrete walls into sympathetic barking. Laurie and I went for an evening walk, finding, as the closest thing to an appealing vista, a '47 Buick ploughed into a gigantic pile of manure sprouting a crown of feral grasses.

We went to bed early, as much from weariness as to psychologically accelerate our time of departure and the outbound crossing of the California line. When we let Shelagh out to relieve herself in the night, she hit an electric fence with her nose, yelped and started the tiny, invisible dogs into a clamor that lasted the rest of the night. In the morning, as we prepared to go, some of the mystery tubbies were glowering at us across the lines of their private property.

We refueled at Flying J truck stops, as they are set up for big rigs like us. You pull up to the pump, pick up a telephone, and explain your attentions to an invisible cashier. When you're finished, you pull forward into your own fifty-five-foot parking space and go inside for food, showers, television, magazines, money machines, video games, telephones, maps, and so on. With the right cards, you could run a modest-size nation from a Flying J truck stop. Flying J seems to have forgotten nothing in serving their customers; though from observation, I don't know why they decided to farm out the tattoos. Oddly enough, Laurie found this atmosphere ominous and disquieting. She spotted a small group seated around a table, intently watching a television set that was not tuned to a station but simply revealed a screenful of loud, hissing snow. She felt that people here were casing each other. She felt it wasn't looking good. In retrospect, this was the beginning of our homesickness for the frozen north.

When you first cross Arizona from California, things are slow to change, and you see things to which you are unaccustomed at home: drive-through zoos, flea markets measured in square miles, pickup trucks hauling exercycles, a huge automobile junkyard served by a Subway sandwich shop, Liz Claiborne outlets, the Harlem Globetrotters tour bus, airborne garbage bags, an aviation graveyard that looks like a major metropolitan airport, the Rooster Cogburn Ostrich Ranch.

We managed to make our way through all of this, out the other side of Tucson, and into the hill country near Mexico where our friends, Peter and Molly Phinny, kindly allowed us to pull our trailer onto their land and use their corrals. Laurie walked around in the mesquite trees with her cell phone trying to find a signal.

When we put our horses into their spacious cedar corrals, it seemed we were meeting them again in surroundings more appropriate to them. They were in the middle of a big country best traversed by horse, and as they wheeled happily around their new place I felt whatever that great feeling is about horses and the country they ought to be in. Today's equestrian contests, whether cuttings, reinings and ropings, or dressage meets, are rather industrial affairs of trucks, trailers, stalls, wheelbarrows, as well as the continual veterinary attentions appropriate to these physically stressed animals. But horses seem to like new country nearly as well as we do. Ours were overwhelmed by their good feeling and began speeding in circles that cast a long cloud of dust adrift over the scrubland.

The next two nights we spent dining at the home of Linda and Jim Harrison in very old friendship. Jim and I abandoned ourselves to the horseplay of forty years' customary habit until the expression of alarm on the face of his youngest daughter, Anna, encouraged us to moderate. We ate good food and talked eagerly of books and birds. Because Linda suffers from asthma, Jim must pursue his frantic cigarette smoking by plunging his upper body into the fireplace where he continues to supply interjections in a voice made sepulchral by the masonry. The door was opened upon a small patio that overlooks a birdy wood where the elegant trogon or vermilion flycatcher could fall to one's eye. I thought the euphoria I felt on these evenings might be part of the wanderer's grace, in which elements of the past and present unexpectedly collide like the Paris saunterings of middle-aged Lakota warriors and ex-cavalrymen in Buffalo Bill's circus.

Possibly being around people in a wheelless home contributed to the further inklings of homesickness. I became more aware that my setter, Gracie, was at home in Montana, and my kelpie, Pat, and our brood mares. I admired, from this distance, the jays and chickadees at our feeders who refrained from bolting to warm climes in the winter.

Our decision to set out for a couple of weeks of living in an area not much larger than the mudroom on the ranch was a plunge into the unknown. To our surprise, we were rising to the challenge. I had developed some housekeeping skills I'd not previously possessed and my faintly obsessive personality found a home in the washing, drying, and storing of dishes. At the onset, we had agreed to view one another's organizational eccentricities in the manner of anthropologists. We tried to take note of these things rather than exception to them. There were new problems of censoriousness as when one gazed with feigned objectivity at the dirty clothes festooning a doorknob. This was fooling no one and eventually we gave it up. Our attention turned to the curious society of laundromats, the renewability of propulsive fuels for the people of the highway, and that most remarkable of conveniences, the free RV-holding tank dump station, the sort of thing that really keeps a marriage together.

We loaded the horses and headed back through Tucson and up to Maricopa, home of several feedlots, including the O.K. Cattle Company. We hauled our trailer into a universe of feeder cattle, hundreds of thousands of them, a genuinely grim scene. The wind howled over this gloomy world and we resorted to routine as we unloaded horses, buckets, rakes, blankets, hooked up all our hookups, and stalled the horses. It was a four-day cutting and we immediately began to win a bit of money, which was heartening; but on the third day the wind died and the smell nearly took the paint off our truck. There was reason to doubt that having our own home in the middle of this was a real plus. Overhead, an array of high tension lines prevented Laurie from getting a good signal though she wandered about with her cell phone like a uranium prospector. I think she wondered whether people who lived like this could really have children and needed electronic confirmation of their existence. At night, nearly everyone left and we were alone with two hundred horses and eight Port-a-potties. On the last run either of us would have before starting home, Laurie and Delta laid down a perfect run, securing a healthy check. Laurie had been working hard toward this accomplishment, the moment when she and her mare were but one individual. When the cutting was over, we gathered up our winnings, loaded our weary horses, and started balling the jack northward. Our friend Lisa Peters met us in the predawn dark with a beautiful plate of road food and we promised to meet in the sandhills of Nebraska in May, with trucks, trailers, horses, and gas-fired barbecues. We failed to note that it was February and we were in our shirtsleeves, the windows down in the truck, as we pushed through Phoenix and Flagstaff and on across the sweeping Navajo reservation, a hundred gallons of Number Two Diesel under our belts, past Indian children herding sheep, Navajo veteran memorials, a museum to the Navajo code talkers of World War Two, a sign that proclaimed "Chief Yellow Horse Loves You!"—we're coming dogs, brood mares, kids!—all the way past the last hogan into Utah, where by a miracle we found comfortable corrals in the heart of Canyonlands. We fed in our coats and made laughing reference to the sunburns we retained from the day before.

The next day we pulled hard, clear across Utah and into Idaho, then up toward the high border country near Montana, whose border crossing we anticipated giddily. By St. Anthony, Idaho, we were driving on packed snow and ice and I noted that there were fewer and fewer souls on the roads. Near Island Park, it was us and a bunch of snowmobiles. Our doubts were growing as the walls of snow built on either side of us. The light levels in mid-afternoon were so low, the snowmobilers had their lights on as they cavorted in the trees. We passed one of their accident scenes, a four-wheel-drive ambulance and a helmeted figure stretched out on the ground under a thermal blanket. As we moved into the northern winter and sundown, I was grateful for the cell phone and our AAA membership.

By the time we crossed into Montana, losing our light and in an intensifying blizzard, pulling thirty-eight feet of house and horses over corrugated ice, I was looking for a place to stop for the night. Laurie crawled into the backseat with her dog, her phone, a bowl of water for the dog, her Flying J popcorn, her paperback, and her Diet Coke. The Madison Valley seemed snowed in and abandoned of even ranch traffic. Small, distant yard lights glowed through the blizzard and I was riveted on what little of the road I could see through the gusting snow.

"You know," I said, "maybe we ought to call in and get a road report. This is looking tough."

"I don't think so."

"What do you mean, you don't think so?"

"I dropped the phone in the dog water. She's dead."

It was true: no amount of holding it in the blast from the heater could resolve the fog in its little window; its dial tone had become the croak of a raven. Getting stuck was not an option. We would keep going forward or be found later, by probe.

We stared down every crawling mile until the familiar glow of Ennis appeared through the storm. I wheeled my way all the way to the rodeo grounds west of town where we dragged the trailer until the snow stopped our progress. We double-blanketed the horses and put them in the bronc pens, which were so drifted in we had to shovel their gates loose. The water hydrant was frozen, so we carried buckets from the trailer in biting, snow-filled wind. The horses turned their butts into it and nosed down into their double rations of hay. We were wondering how a couple of empty nesters could get themselves into a place like this. "What were we thinking?" Laurie asked of no one in particular.

A sign at the entrance to the rodeo grounds stated that it was necessary to have permission to stall horses here; the sign gave a phone number. But our phone didn't work. So, I climbed a fence and trudged toward the lights of a house across the snowy field. I knocked on the door, startling the older couple I saw sitting in the living room. They looked at each other hesitantly before answering. The woman came to the door and I explained my situation, asking to use the phone. I got permission to use the corrals and when I hung up, the old woman said, "Where are you staying?" I told her about the living quarters in our trailer. "Not on a night like this," she said emphatically. "You go get your wife and stay here. We have a nice spare bedroom." I explained that we would be very comfortable where we were. "Well, if you're not, you come right back here. I don't care what time of the night it is."

I thanked her and walked back to the trailer. Even the snow felt warm.

9
A FOAL

It isn't really summer until the shelter belt on the east side of the corrals leafs out. That makes all the difference because it blocks the sun in the first corral. It is also the time when, if you sit in the ancient Crow vision-quest site on the western side of the ranch, you will see the sun rise at the center of the valley in a remarkable suggestion of the first light of the world.

I had three mares confined. Two had already had their colts and the third, my adored quarter horse Lu-Lu, was three weeks late and very uncomfortable. The saddle horses, five geldings, including two venerated pensioners in their twenties, stayed close to the corrals in their pasture because they were interested in these births and had proven to be doting uncles over the years. But in the summertime at first light, they were usually lying down asleep in the sun. Nothing moved, not even their tails, because it was still too cool for flies.

I usually get up early and head to the bunkhouse, where I work. I don't always go straight in there as I try to suggest by my brisk departure. I worried that in that building, hunched over a legal pad still in the trance of sleep, I might feel irony was required and it was much too early for that; though in the early quiet, it is often to big issues one's mind wanders, guilt at all this tranquility, the feeling that I and my work had been diminished by thirty years of rusticating among the Missouri's smallest headwaters. At such times, I console myself with some literary anecdote like Mencken's remark that he didn't care how well Willa Cather wrote, he wasn't interested in anything that happened in Nebraska, a remark that blew up in Mencken's face like an exploding cigar. Or, I think of the ways Montaigne got everyone to visit him in the boondocks. And so on and so forth. I was carrying my coffee. A small river whispers around the edge of the yard and down behind the barn, a sparkling freestone river that springs from a mountain range I can see to the south. Its height changes daily according to melt-off and storms in the mountains, events I couldn't detect; but I can see the dark rings around the stones when the river is falling, the shells of transforming stoneflies, the dart of yellow warblers crossing the river to their willow nests.

LuLu had not been happy, not eating, strangely unimpressed by the snacks I kept in my coat, and after two weeks her broodiness had infected me. When I reached under to feel her taut udder, its heat and softness were pronounced; she pretended to lift a leg toward me with an annoyed grunt but I knew it was because she was sore. Her foal liked one side of her body one day and the next was on the other, pushing a knee around the side of LuLu's stomach. LuLu laid her ears back close to her head at this provocation. It did seem that the nipples had faintly exuded some wax, which, just ahead of the colostrum, could mean imminent birth. LuLu was the tenderest of animals, though in her days as a cutting horse, she could astonish with her bursts of speed and hard, sliding stops. She mourned for six weeks when a friend of hers, a cat, went to another ranch to mouse. So, her stoniness toward me at this late hour of her confinement was disquieting.

One morning, I made my accustomed feint toward the place of work and irony, and went to the corrals. The geldings were asleep in the pasture, except for the most avuncular of them, Lucky Bottom 79. LuLu no longer consorted with the mares who already had their colts. Instead, she stood in the shade of the caragana bushes without any movement. She was thinner all right, but she looked alone. I went to her with a chill of fear; the speed of birth in horses is such that things go wrong quickly. But when I was a few paces away, a small head popped up and regarded me; the foal was almost invisible against the ground and LuLu nickered to me. The afterbirth was on the ground a couple of yards away. I lifted it up and inspected it for completeness. Glistening, startlingly heavy, and still warm, the afterbirth was shaped like the bottom of a pair of long underwear with one leg shorter than the other. Any dog worthy of the name, like my three, considers this a windfall of immaculate protein.

When I knelt by the foal, an exquisite sorrel filly, her head nodded up and down and she made several attempts to stand. Her tiny black hooves were just beginning to harden. LuLu buried her nostrils in my hair to reconfirm my identity and let me examine the little horse, who presently heaved herself onto sprawled legs wobbling and erect. Arms around her torso, her coat warm and dry, eyes big as a deer's, the beat of her heart coming through her rib cage as she yearned toward LuLu's udder, I steadied her until the connection was made and I saw the pumping movement in her throat.

A new horse.